ABOUT THE AUTHOR OF THIS BOOK

José Antonio Burciaga was raised in the West Texas border town of El Paso. He is a seasoned Chicano cultural activist, muralist, humorist and founding member of the comedy group Culture Clash. He now lives in Monterey. His book *Undocumented Love* (Chusma House) won the Before Columbus American Book Award for poetry. He is also the author of *Drink Cultura: Chicanismo* (Joshua Odell Editions).

SPILLING THE BEANS

SPILLING THE BEANS

LOTERÍA CHICANA

JOSÉ ANTONIO BURCIAGA

Joshua Odell Editions
SANTA BARBARA

NOTE

This book has been reasonably priced for use in the classroom. Please, no photocopying.

Published by Joshua Odell Editions

Box 2158, Santa Barbara, CA 93120

ACKNOWLEDGEMENTS

Two essays in this collection originally appeared in the following publications, to whose editors and publishers thank are due.
"The Taxicab Brigade," *METRO, San Jose Weekly,* July 8-14, 1993.
"La Sanitaria," *Puerto Del Sol,* New Mexico State University, Spring 1990.

LIBRARY OF CONGRESS CATALOG CARD NUMBER: 95-068912
ISBN 1-877741-11-6

Book Design/Typesetting by George Delmerico

Printed in the United States of America

APPRECIATION

Cecilia Preciado Burciaga

Rafael Jesús Gonzalez

Irma Herrera

Francisco Morales

José Novoa

Virginia Tapia

TO THE LOVE AND MEMORY OF

María Margarita Burciaga

12 MARCH 1950 — 8 FEBRUARY 1995

PRECIOUS SISTER, MOTHER, AUNT, FRIEND, AND TEACHER

Her life like a flower, ephemeral but
beautiful, here for an instant and gone
too soon...leaving behind the
fragrance of her memory.
She lives through her sons,
Oscar, Aaron, her brothers, sisters,
the people she knew and loved,
the students she taught,
the truths she taught,
the things she touched...

CONTENTS

SPILLING THE BEANS

"Eat your beans!" I hated beans, I ate them all the time. We had beans in the morning, at noon and at night.

"Eat your beans!" "Finish your beans!" We ate them freshly made *frijoles de la olla,* we ate them in different recipes: *frijoles borrachos, frijoles charros, frijoles sencillos* . . . We ate *enfrijoladas,* like enchiladas but soaked in beans instead of chile, we had *tacos de frijoles,* bean burritos, tostadas de burritos, refried bean sandwiches and even matzohs or bagels smothered with refried beans. We scrambled them with eggs, we ate them with diced jalapeños, nopalitos, chorizo, melted cheese . . . You name it. We ate *frijoles* when its soup thickened. We ate them when the refried beans had just about dried up.

Enter any Mexican home and you can tell by the smell if there is a fresh pot of beans on the stove. The aroma is unmistakable. A pot of freshly made beans is a delectable dish. Well cooked, beans will just about melt in your mouth. Immediately after cooking, add oregano, cilantro, onions, or even Parmesan cheese to individual servings for an exquisite culinary experience. For many of us, it is our invariable soup du jour. Some people will add a can of beer when the beans are cooking. And the second time they are warmed up some people add milk or cream or cheese.

But somehow, grandmother's beans always tasted better, and my Mother's were also good but different from my aunts' and my mother-in- law's. It was the water! Or a mystery that will forever remain a *secreto*. And there were times when my Mexican aunts would open up a quart of beans the way you opened a glass liter of milk. Some entrepreneur began marketing it as an indispensable common staple like milk.

And once in a while my mother made them my favorite way, as a dessert, as a sweet pudding, similar to chocolate. Gently cooking them with sugar instead of salt, she blended them and added cinnamon and a touch of vanilla, sometimes raisins. It was better than chocolate pudding. Beans were not only economical but versatile. However, we did have a choice at mealtime: It was eat them or *nada!*

We also feasted on many other kinds of legumes such as *lentejas,* which my mother called *frijolitos del niño Dios,* because Baby Jesus was supposed to have eaten them. How could we refuse? There were navy beans, garbanzos, lima beans, kidney beans, black beans and pinto beans. Whether we liked them or not, we ate them all.

Easy to prepare, the most essential and critical part was to thoroughly clean them of hard little rocks that could easily demolish your molars, incisors or front teeth. But beans also had fun uses. Small bean bags were fun to throw and play catch with. Pea shooters had their season. Beans were what we played Lotería with, the Mexican bingo game. *"¡El Cazo!"* And we would put a pinto bean on that picture.

Beans could also be dangerous. Little kids would put a dry pinto bean up their nose. Sometimes they said nothing until the bean softened, grew and sprouted like a sponge, then had to be extracted by the family doctor.

While I was being forced to eat my beans, little Johnny and Susie were being forced to eat their spinach. As the All-American vegetable, it was supposed to make them strong like Popeye the Sailor Man. In Crystal City, Texas, the supposed spinach capitol of the world and a stronghold of Chicano activism in the late sixties, they even erected a statue of Popeye.

I liked spinach, but no one ever told us that beans packed more power than spinach. We should have brought out Freddy Frijol who would have whipped Popeye. The difference at the Battle of the Alamo was the difference between *espinacas* and frijoles. Mexico won! Remember the Alamo!

High in iron, beans form an essential part of the mechanism in the blood that helps supply oxygen to body cells, aids in respiration and energy production. It's also an excellent source of fiber, and rich in minerals, including calcium, phosphorus, magnesium, niacin, thiamine, riboflavin, B vitamins and zinc. It helps in blood clotting. Beans, *frijoles,* legumes, those dehydrated pods of edible food that turn soft and nutritious when cooked go back to the Bronze Age, thus the reason for our color. A couple of thousand years before Christ, they were already grown by Egyptians who claimed they had a mystical power and offered them in their rituals to the deceased.

The Romans determined the guilt or innocence of a man on trial with beans. Jurors would cast a white bean for innocence and a black or red bean for guilt. The status of beans among Romans is found in the names of a prominent ancient family: Fabius was named after the Faba bean, Lentulus was named after the lentil, Piso from the pea and the most distinguished Cicero was named after the chick pea.

Then there was Judge Roy Bean (1825?-1904) a West Texas saloon keeper, coroner and justice of the peace on the West Texas frontier. He had his hands full with his six guns and a town filled with gamblers, rustlers and thieves. He was the "Law West of the Pecos," who once fined a corpse $40 for carrying a concealed weapon. In more modern times, another Texan, U.S. astronaut Alan Lavern Bean, piloted the lunar module Intrepid on the Apollo 12 mission and in November of '69 made man's second moon landing. Last but not least is my friend Frijol who has yet to do anything of such magnitude but, his life isn't over.

One historical dish stands out: *Moros y Cristianos,* Moors and Christians. That's what you call a plate of white rice and black beans, referring to the African Moors who occupied white Spain for close to 800 years until they were expelled in 1492. In Nicaragua, a similar dish is called *Gallo Pinto.*

Other Spanish names for frijoles abound: *frejoles, judias de león, habichuelas, alubias,* and *habas.* As kids we would change frijoles to a more Chicano sounding *firoles* or *balas; un plato de balas* was a deadly "plate of bullets." Beans are rich in nutrition but many people shy away from them because of their gas producing properties, something that can easily be remedied. (One way is to repeatedly discard the water. First, let the beans soak temporarily or overnight and then throw out the water. Boil them and throw out the water again. When adding new water, boil it first if you want your pinto beans to retain a pink color, otherwise they turn dark. Another remedy is to use a commercial food additive known as Beano and follow their directions. *Muy importante!*)

Long thought to be the staple of peasants, who would have thought they would be served in fancy restaurants or banquets? Imagine a *maitre d'* reciting the soup du jour as *frijoles de la olla* or a *pate de refritos.* But there are very exclusive restaurants that serve these dishes. Between San Francisco and San Diego it has become part of the new California cuisine.

Some people eat chicken and burp beans, so goes the Mexican proverb, *Comen pollo y erutan frijoles!* From the children's story about Jack and the Beanstalk to Miguel de Cervantes Saavedra's immortal *Don Quixote de la Mancha*, beans have risen to the highest levels of the literary classics.

Native to North and South America, many beans were domesticated by the Incas of Peru. Easier to cultivate in poorer soil than corn they can be dried and stored for long periods of time.

But the beans that will spill from this book are beans that have boiled for over 500 years. Not a melting pot but a kettle filled with black beans, white beans, red kidney beans, cranberry beans, coffee beans, navy beans and pinto beans.

Spilling the beans is about disclosing, divulging, revealing, confessing and publishing pods of truth, facts of integrity, humor and pathos. Spilling them hell! We are throwing them up in the air.

EL DIABLO Y EL MAMBO

It was a dry and hot June day in '52 when *El Diablo* danced its way to the Northern edge of the Chihuahuan desert. That's what they called the tiny twisters that raised a swirl of dust across the desert floor. The priest knew and the *viejos* knew El Diablo had screwed its way up from hell. It was the same day *el mambo* had blown in on the radio airwaves from the big Mexican city on the border. The latest dance craze pranced in like a mad passionate ballet, like the scrawny little desert twisters of sand alongside tumbling tumbleweeds.

El mambo had danced its way into the hearts and minds of Samalayuca's youth and unpaved streets. The dance was suggestive, primitive and sinful as a harlot on the border.

Padre Pelayo was the first to publicly denounce the music and the dance. Padre Pelayo was burning angry the Sunday morning he climbed the squeaky stairs to the high pulpit and angrily bellowed in the cavernous adobe church. "*¡Esa música es imoral, degenerada y satánica!* Anyone dancing to that music will automatically be excommunicated, *en el nombre del Santísimo Pontífice, y todos los Santos del cielo! Es* the work of the devil himself! El boogie was bad enough. *Gracias a Dios,* el boogie never caught on! But now this! The people and the nation know better! May *Dios* have *misericordia* on your souls!" His words echoed and reverberated from the ancient adobe walls of the dusty church and the faithful feared his words and the possibility that the priest's scarlet puffed face would trigger *un ataque cardiaco.*

It was the gravest moral issue Samalayuca had ever encountered. The older people understood and scolded their grandchildren and children. They had seen the writing on the wall. The young people disagreed. How could music and dance come from the devil? But that was not a question to ask Padre Pelayo. Only heretics and *estúpidos* would ever ask such a simple question of Padre Pelayo.

El mambo was still a satanic novelty when it claimed its first victim. It happened at a Saturday night dance in the only dance hall that served as a restaurant during the day. The only good thing about Samalayuca was their weekly Saturday night dances. Even men and women from the big city of Juarez came, sometimes. On that night, the young men wore white dress shirts, dark pants and *Brillantina de Rosas* on their hair. Young *señoritas* helped set each other's hair or borrowed each other's shoes, dresses, a ribbon or perfume.

There was something about the mambo that had attracted the young Mexicanos from Mexico City to Samalayuca. *Muy Latino y tropical!* It had a modern, hot and sultry big band sound. Even the titles of the numbers, such as Mambo Numero Cinco was *suave.*

The young victim's name was María. ". . . and with a name like that!" the priest had shouted to his parishioners.

Saturday night, María arrived early at the dance hall, more than ready for a fun time. No one in Samalayuca loved to dance like María and everyone knew it. That afternoon she had practiced el mambo with Elsa, her best friend. María walked into the hall, ready and poised, with a feminine gait to hide a hint of high heel insecurity.

"Will they play the mambo?" one of her friends asked. *¡Seguro que si!"*—"Of course!" another echoed angrily.

"Well," María said, " I am ready to dance with the devil himself. The other women laughed as they stood in a small circle, talking and surveying the available men without so much as letting one of them know what they were doing.

The music started and a tall young man walked in. No one knew him but that was not unusual. Young men from the agricultural college in Juarez frequently came to the *baile.* The only unusual thing about this man were his good looks. The women took note, faintly took a second look and then gave each other knowing glances of approval and desire.

The first number was a mambo and the young man approached María. With nothing more than a bowed request in his eyes, María gently nodded yes, took his hand, and walked to the dance floor. There were other couples on the floor but María and the young man were unique. They were a made to order couple, and it was as if they had danced together many times before. She smiled and in between their movements she stole glances at the young man whose riveting eyes never left her.

El Bato was, as we say, *más moreno que wachuseh*—darker than what you say. And he was so cool in the style of those *batos* that are with "¡it!"—who know the etiquette of his people, who treat women right, are tough with other batos and smart without showing "¡it!" María was a dark beauty, the kind you long for right away, long black hair, lithe, and *firme* in the most beautiful way you wanna know. She was so tiny that she had to dance on her tip toes yet accompanied her *compañero* so gracefully that Fred Astaire would've tripped over with jealousy. The bato had the just-right *greña,* mop of hair, white T-Shirt, jeans and he could dance like there was no *mañana.* With his left hand he gently held his María's tiny waist while the other arm kind of just limply hung down with his thumb stuck in his front jeans pocket. He was on the slim side and the pronounced veins on his forearms told everyone he labored hard. He was like a Mexican James Dean. And she was just plain decent like no one to be compared to. Who knew what his name was. Nobody knew and nobody cared because they were kind of lost in each other and el mambo. Like they were so natural they weren't really concentrating or listening but feeling it.

The next number was a real cool *número* because the dancers kind of trotted like ponies with the woman riding on the guy's thigh, which can raise more than your heart-beat and eyebrows.

On the slower números they danced cheek to cheek, French kissed and passed chewing gum to each other, interspersed with sweet delicious lies that go to the heart, "Ooooh Baby! *Te quiero chingos!* ¡Oooh Baby! ¡Ayyyyy! " He hissssssssed, she closed her eyes and pressed closer as the *caballito* trotted faster.

They moved and writhed in the most natural and sensuous ways to the rhythm, to the beat, to the tempo, to the heart, unaware they were an inspiration, a classic living, breathing, dancing sculpture.

The dance number ended, the dancers clapped, thanked each other, and walked away from the dance floor. María and this *bato* waited for the next dance.

"¡It was El Mambo Número Cinco!" They both laughed and began dancing. María was in heaven. He was a terrific dancing partner, *guapo,* and had a quiet but pleasant personality that was charming.

After the mambo they both stopped to catch their breath.

"Would you like something to drink?" the young man asked María.

"That would be wonderful!" María responded, realizing

her heart was beating fast with exhilaration. She fanned herself with her hand as he left for the soda. As he made his way through the crowd, María was overcome with heat, went limp and then softly fainted to the floor.

People swarmed around her until someone yelled, "Make room! Move away! She needs air!"

Elsa noticed the commotion around where María had been dancing and broke through the crowd to find her friend on the floor and a heavy older man fanning her and asking for water, space and air. Elsa flushed with slight anger recalling María had come to the dance without anything to eat the whole day. So much preparation and excitement for the day to end like this.

María did not revive. The music stopped. They brought water, made space, fanned her, poured water into her mouth, and put a wet handkerchief on her forehead. But María would not respond. Samalayuca had no doctor, only dos *parteras,* wet nurses and one *curandera* who lived in the *pueblo.* One *policia* decided to drive María to Juarez along with Elsa.

The *policia* picked her up from the floor and felt her warm body. When he stood up with her across his arms, the crowd gasped as they noticed the imprint of a man's hand on her back. The women led out shrill gasps of horror. The men groaned. Someone leaned over to tell the *policia* carrying María, and the man's face lit up with horror. He gained his composure and walked to the police car.

The handsome young bato disappeared into the desert night never to be seen again.

The story spread like wild fire, reaching the hospital before they did. The rumor crossed the border into El Chuco.

Everyone was shocked, except Padre Pelayo. He had known all along the consequences and the power of Satan! El mambo had claimed its first victim. Young women everywhere heard the story. But by then the mambo had already caught on.

LA SANITARIA

My *carnal,* Pifas, and I received thirty-five cents apiece every two weeks from mamá, who insisted we get a haircut that often, lest we look *mechudos,* shaggy. That was forty-some years ago.

Haircuts in El Chuco were a dollar so we crossed the border to Juaritos, Chihuahua, Mexico, where they were only 25 cents. That left ten cents each to get there and return on the bus and *tranvía,* the trolley car. To pay the El Paso

City Lines ten cents was a waste when we could walk free, to and from Juarez and buy candy. Nobody walks anymore and the El Paso City Lines is now named SCAT which stands for Sun City Area Transit but really means Scattering Chicanos Across Town.

Back then, *everything* was cheaper in Juarez. Our barbershop was named La Sanitaria although it was not all that sanitary, but it was clean, if you know what I mean. La Sanitaria was on Avenida Juarez right in the middle of the Juarez red light district, close to the bridge.

In broad sunlight Pifas and I passed all the strip tease joints with the black and white glossy photos of buxomed peroxide blondes and pushy doormen like Buddy Cachetón from the Chinese Palace who urged or pushed all passers inside.

But to walk inside La Sanitaria was sometimes more intimidating. The barbers were men with nothing but sex on their minds and a comment on every young woman that passed by the front window. The waiting chairs had various raggedy, sepia-colored issues of *Policia* and *Escándalo* magazines. The floor was black and white checkered tile with black hair strewn around each of the ten barber chairs. And of course you could always tell by the blonde hair when a *huero* had been there, not necessarily a Gringo. It was always full on Saturday afternoons.

Luckily there weren't that many people that one Saturday when I was determined to get my hair cut the way God commanded. Crowned with two serious cow-licks my hair would stick up when it was cut too short. I looked like a rooster so at night my mother would make me wear a nylon cap to press the cow-licks down so that the next day I would not look like the Mexican—"What me worry?"—kid, Alfredo E. Neuman.

My turn came up after Pifas was already getting his haircut. I sat up in the chair and in a loud authoritative voice that traveled across the long room I told the barber in Spanish "*No me corte de arriba porque se me para.*" That translated to "Don't cut any off the top so my hair won't stand up." But the way it came off in Spanish was "Don't cut any off the top or I will get an erection."

The ten barbers and the very short and fat bald owner at the cash register had the laugh of the week. My face, sticking out of the white cloth, flushed red as a tomato. I could do nothing but smile weakly and wish I was ten miles North under my bed.

After paying two *cuiras* for both haircuts, we walked away brushing the loose bits of hair that pricked as they fell down our necks. With each step North, I felt better.

But we had to walk back home past El Segundo Barrio. It was the toughest neighborhood in El Chuco. Though Pifas and I did it all the time, we were cautious always looking at least a block ahead and behind us knowing exactly where to turn and run.

We passed the barrio, El Alcazar and El Colón movie theaters without incident. El Colón was the Mexican movie house that premiered all the Pedro Infante and Cantinflas films. El Alcazar across the street was the only movie theater for the few El Paso Blacks. Chicanos also frequented this movie theater which we called El Calcetín, The Sock, because of its aroma.

We were always a little apprehensive walking past El Segundo and so as we neared the downtown area we began to relax. But that was not to be our day. As we passed the Palace Theater that was forever showing Leo Gorcey and his Bowery Gang movies, someone called me a bow-legged *hijo de* so and so. Besides the two cow-licks I was also bow-legged. I turned to see this young *chuco* who was nothing but a kid. We couldn't believe this little *bato* had the *huevos.* Pifas and I turned around and slowly walked up to him. All of a sudden he turned scared and backed into a parked car. Feeling the power and ease with which we had cornered this punk we almost didn't notice the gleam of a knife in his hand.

"Watch out! He's got a knife." I froze for a second and then noticed as he began to fold it away. The young chuco had been glancing back and forth to a corner a few feet away. I glanced sideways to see what he was looking at. Sure enough, his *camaradas* turned the corner. A whole mob of them. They were taller and older. A trap, an ambush!

And they were almost on top of us before we took off running.

We ran, like we had never run before. As it was, we were fast. They could never catch us. We ran like speeding bullets through the downtown area, dodging, running into people and cars, turning back and watching them drop off except for the tallest, lankiest and meanest looking. Pifas and I stayed together as we ran through the Plazita with the alligator pond. That's where we lost the last of them.

With hearts pounding from the one-mile run and ten cents in each of our pockets we had survived another haircut and celebrated at Mac's News stand with a Barq's soda and a candy bar.

We had survived another journey into our mother country, gotten a haircut and crossed enemy territory. We clinked soda bottles in a toast, safe for another two weeks before our next adventure. It was all in the name of economics and decent appearances.

RAMBLINGS ON NAFTA

The North American Free Trade Agreement between Canada, Mexico and the United States is an idea that goes back to prehistoric times when indigenous peoples traversed the longitude of the continent migrating, exchanging and bartering for food, furs, shells, and precious stones. But as a formal agreement between countries, one of the first proposals was voiced by an early Californio in the early 1860's.

Once upon a time—like over a hundred years

ago—there lived a Spanish General in California whose name was Mariano Guadalupe Vallejo. Unlike the city named after him, pronounced Va-lay-hoe, the General's name is pronounced Va-ye-ho. The first settler to be awarded a Spanish land grant in Alta California, Vallejo had requested this grant to offset the encroaching Russian whaling stations along the upper California and Northwest coast.

In the back-room of a dusty antique book store in Monterey, California, I ran across the following anecdote in a thin pamphlet entitled "The Rambling Sketches and Experiences of 64 Years of Litt. Wooley," a member of the Society of California Pioneers & Vigilante Committee of 1856. Published in 1913 the pamphlet covers the period from 1849 to 1913,

During the early part of the Civil War President Abraham Lincoln called General Mariano Guadalupe Vallejo to Washington on business. During their conversations, General Vallejo suggested to President Lincoln that the United States build a railroad into Mexico, believing as he said, "it would be a benefit to both nations."

A smiling President Lincoln asked, "What good would it do for our people to go down to Mexico even if the railroad were built? They would all die of fever and according to your belief, go down yonder," with a motion of his hand towards the supposed location of the infernal fires.

"I wouldn't be very sorry about that," General Vallejo answered coolly.

"How so?" President Lincoln asked, "I thought you liked the Yankees."

"So I do," was the answer. "The Yankees are a wonderful people! Wonderful! Wherever they go they make improvements. If they were to emigrate in large number to hell itself, they would somehow manage to change the climate."

This first recorded attempt at a trade agreement between Mexico and the United States becomes an interesting historical anecdote that preceded NAFTA. It was perhaps the first diplomatic clash over trade agreement between an Anglo-American and an Indo-Hispanic country.

A more recent clash occurred on the first day of 1994, when NAFTA was to take effect, the dawn of a new commercial day when Mexico was to join the new world industrial order. The Zapatista Army of the indigenous peoples of Chiapas rebelled against NAFTA, Article 27 of the Mexican Constitution, poverty and oppression.

According to Chiapas union organizer José Juarez, when President Carlos Salinas retired for the night on New Year's Eve, he thought "he would wake up a North American. But instead he woke up a Guatemalan."

The indigenous revolution protested a trade agreement that threatened them with extinction. As small agricultural producers they saw NAFTA as the "death certificate" for over one million Chiapanecos. They called for more sensitive economic programs that guaranteed their indigenous way of life.

NAFTA came as a post-Soviet North American program to expand the technocratic industrial markets. But indigenous and Western economic philosophies clashed. An indigenous lifestyle tied to the land clashed with an industrial style that threatened to bring cycles of urban crime, poverty, mass migration to cities, to *El Norte* and ecological disasters. Coffee, cattle and corn prices had spiraled down. Very few campesinos owned small parcels of land. Campesinos were banned from cutting down trees. Meanwhile, the Mexican government had cut aid programs for farms and reduced agricultural, credit and technical assistance.

But the painful dilemma in Chiapas had less to do with trade than it did with poverty. More than one million Indigenous Chiapanecos who make up one-third of the population live in extreme poverty on the worst lands in the most inaccessible parts of Mexico with the fewest social services, schools or clinics.

However, NAFTA was not the lone cause for rebellion. The Mexican government's decision in 1991 to amend Article 27 of the Mexican Constitution was just as responsible. Since 1917 Article 27 had obliged the state to redistribute land to any petitioner who fulfilled the necessary legal requirements. The main category of campesino land-ownership was the *ejido,* an area made up of individual plots and communal property, none of which could be legally sold, rented or used as collateral until the 1991 reforms.

The *ejidos* were formed from the break-up of private estates and the colonization of unused land. Then there are *comunidades agrarias,* lands reclaimed by Indian villages from private owners who had encroached on their holdings in the late nineteenth and early twentieth centuries. These campesino land-holdings were threatened when Article 27 allowed private companies of at least 25 individuals to own larger parcels of land. Article 27 allowed the use of land as collateral, thus the risk of foreclosures and loss of land rights. A backlog of unresolved land petitions ran the risk of being rejected.

It was eerie. On 1 January 1994, Mexico slipped back into the Revolution of 1910 and Emiliano Zapata was again fighting for *tierra, libertad y justicia.* This was not far from the truth. Mexico's Revolution of 1910 never reached Chiapas. For many Chiapanecos Emiliano Zapata is not a namesake but a real live figure who still rides throughout the *campos.*

Subcomandante Marcos, the mysterious masked leader and spokesperson, was not the commander but a *subcomandante,* not indigenous but of more European extraction and culture. Nonetheless, an American in the hemispheric sense of the word.

The dilemmas that run through Chiapas, Article 27, NAFTA, the Zapatistas, and Subcomandante Marcos are too complex to expound on. But historical anecdotes and metaphors can serve as parables for future shocks.

Mexico is home to the largest population of Indigenous people on this continent. Chiapas is at the epicenter of the American Indian population in Mesoamerica with over one million indigenous Chiapanecos. The power and influence of the Mesoamerican peoples through their growing population and network across the continent will continue to be felt. They have come down from the mountain in more ways than one.

If 1992 marked 500 years of European colonialism, it also

marked the beginning of another cycle of change.

The year 1492 not only marked the encounter between two worlds, it also marked the expulsion of the Moors from Spain after 800 years occupation. Eight hundred years is longer than a short Quincentennary when comparing the Moorish occupation of Spain to the European occupation of America.

Before the Moors, the Romans controlled Spain for 400 years. Other groups that left their imprint on Spain were the Iberians, Ligurians, Celts, Phoenicians, Carthaginians, Visigoths, Jews, followed by the Arabs and then the Moors. They didn't leave Spain altogether but left a wealth and mixture of cultures. The last were the Moors and their influence remains to this date in Spanish culture. Most words beginning with *al* have an Arabic origin: *alcazar* (castle), *almohada* (pillow), *alberca* (pool), *alcancía* (bank) ...words of wealth and comfort. *Alabar* (praise) comes from the Latin and *aleluya* comes from Hebrew. Consider the number of Indian words that now form part of the Spanish and English languages. For the most part, they were words that had to do with the earth and sustenance: potato, tomato, maize, tamal, pizcar (reap) ...

The point is that Euro-American history is too nearsighted and the concept of European time is constrained when compared to the indigenous concept of time. According to the Aztec Calendar, the fifth sun began on the day Cortez entered Mexico City and ended on or about 1992. The Sixth Sun on the Aztec Calendar promises to be positive and beneficial to the Indigenous nations.

This is not an allusion to the end or expulsion of Euroamericans but to the tenacious perseverance and regeneration of Indigenous America. How the American Indian will survive and change us. How Mexico must resolve its crisis of identity. Mexico is more indigenous than it actually believes and practices. It can praise and sing forever about its 30,000 years of splendor but they are hollow words unless they live up to their identity, roots, and their indigenous population.

We are living these changes daily, through cycles and the indomitable spirit of immigrants, all with a legitimate and traditional right to traverse the land on which they live. For in the end, we are all immigrants, here on this earth for only a flash in time.

MAN PROPOSES AND GOD DISPOSES

El hombre propone y Dios dispone

According to an old Spanish proverb, Proposition 187 is waiting for God's disposal. The controversial 1994 California plan to deny certain benefits and services to undocumented immigrants got snagged in the courts despite the majority vote and the media hype, hoopla, hip hoorays and hullabaloos. Some lids just don't fit some jars and the beans keep spilling in.

The whole country is riled up about immigration so man proposes and God disposes: Build a wall; install stadium lights; use infra-red binoculars, television, civilian vigilante squads, national identification cards; dig 15 mile deep ditches; increase border patrol personnel, budgets; call the federal troops and space them 25 yards apart. Yet the people keep coming in biblical proportions. I'm dead sure it's prophesied in the Bible somewhere. To quote a San Diego T-Shirt, "No Problema!"—Polite Spanish meaning, "You have a big problem!"

California Senator Diane Feinstein, former mayor of San Francisco, proposed charging everyone crossing the international bridge an extra dollar or two. Without a clue, President Clinton supported the idea until border politicians explained what it would do to the local economies, penalizing the border for an international problem and having them pay for an international infrastructure. Maybe Clinton and Feinstein thought the Santa Fe Bridge, or the Cordoba Bridge or the Zaragoza Bridges in El Paso were like the Golden Gate Bridge. No way, Josefina!

Some people live on both sides of the border at the same time. Some go back and forth, living temporarily on one side and then the other. Some even have two homes, one on each side of the border. I have a cousin who was born in El Paso, but lived all of his life in Juarez, and then served in the U.S. military.

Mexican mothers rush to have their babies born on the U.S. side of the border not just necessarily for free hospital delivery but because they also want to guarantee their children a hassle free life, like most U.S. Citizens. With U.S.

citizenship you can cross bridges easier and be assured of an education, work and social security. I have friends who grew up on both sides of the border and are now more bilingual, bicultural and binational than wachuseh.

A grand uncle who lived in the central Mexican state of Zacatecas emigrated to El Paso in order to escape the Mexican Revolution of 1910 because he was a pacifist, like his father and grandfather. Two of his boys were born and educated on this side of the border until World War II broke out. Then, my grand uncle moved back to Mexico rather than send his sons to war. They grew up in Juarez, where they to live happily and with successful careers.

Immigration has been a two way street. Forgotten are the poor middle class Euro Americans who retire in Guadalajara, Mexico City, San Miguel Allende among other places. They sometimes form their own communities and even keep to themselves in a form of economic segregation, not unlike the barrios in this country.

In the beginning, President Clinton and Senator Feinstein described Proposition 187 as "mean-spirited" when it sought to deny health and education benefits to children. Then they jumped on the bandwagon when they realized how popular it was.

However, it was so mean-spirited that it caught Texans by surprise. Since losing at the Alamo, Texans have always maintained a notoriously uneasy relationship with Mexico. But they were so shocked at California's Prop. 187, Texans sent their sympathies to Mexico. Of course, they were also luring the California business that Mexico was boycotting.

Texas and California could learn from New Mexico. A couple of years before Proposition 187, the complexities of border crossings and educating Mexican children came to a head in the small border town of Columbus, New Mexico. Isolated in the middle of the desert, Columbus is famous for being the last U.S. territory invaded by a foreign force. On March 9, 1916, Pancho Villa's northern revolutionary forces attacked the town to embarrass the Mexican government's political relations with the U.S. Columbus is so small that the town's outskirts stop at the international line where Palomas, Chihuahua begins.

Phoebe Watson, a Columbus resident (now 84 years young) remembers the Villa attack. Forty-five years ago in 1950 she was principal at Columbus Elementary school and extended an invitation to the Mexican children of Palomas, Chihuahua, to attend Columbus Elementary School. Today, more than 450 students cross the border daily where a yellow bus takes them to the Columbus Elementary School.

Forty-three years passed before a Columbus taxpayer complained about this and filed a lawsuit. Why should New Mexico taxpayers pay for the education of students who live outside the country? This sounded perfectly logical.

However, Phoebe Watson, bless her kind soul, was adamant in her justification. Simply put, it was a very humanitarian and noble act. She put into practice those three virtues this country seemed to have forgotten: faith, hope and charity. "I love the kids," Phoebe Watson declares. "I see absolutely no reason for not educating every child in the world, if you can do it. And we can do it. If we don't teach the children, we lose the world."

Even after the controversy and Proposition 187, Palomas' children continue to cross and attend Columbus Elementary school. Retired, but still active, Phoebe Watson remains adamant, "As a teacher I have a professional obligation to teach children." Who can argue against this high and moral principle? The court threw out the lawsuit due to conflicts between local and state educational jurisdictions and the obligation of schools to educate every child that steps on its front doors.

Of course, Phoebe understands the overcrowding of schools and resources due to the influx of immigrants but she does not swerve from her commitment to educating children. The elementary school in Palomas is the same as many other schools in Mexico, understaffed, with scarce resources and open for only half a day in order to accommodate the same number of students in the afternoon. Phoebe Watson sees Palomas and Columbus as one community, not two.

The international demarcation between two towns isolated in the middle of the desert is artificial and more imaginary than real.

Soon after the first crisis two years ago, fifteen children were refused entry into Columbus Elementary because there were no more desks or space. Phoebe Watson called Carlos Viramontes, the Luna County Superintendent of Schools. The next day space and desks were made available.

Primary concern for a child's education became a priority for this community. One Columbus woman founded a private pre-school care in her own home and named it "Los Amiguitos," admitting children from both countries.

Meanwhile, Luna County Superintendent of Schools, Carlos Viramontes, is looking into opening a binational school with the help of Mexican and U.S. government aid, grants, and private donations. It's nothing new. An international school already exists in Miami, Florida, founded through a treaty with Spain. It is undecided on which side of the border the little international school will be located but it doesn't make any difference in those two communities.

The big boys like President Clinton, Governor Pete Wilson, and their Republican and Democratic cliques would do themselves and the country a big favor by studying one little community in two countries. Columbus Elementary School is teaching children, regardless of their documentation or lack of, instead of making them innocent victims. Should they be interested, it's called "international cooperation" or "teaching children."

THE FIRST THANKSGIVINGS

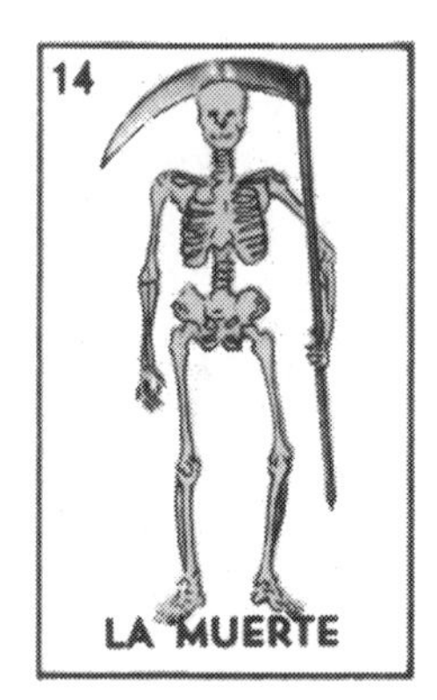

I used to think Thanksgiving was one of the most cherished holidays this country has. The least commercialized, it is the one day of the year when we give thanks to the Almighty for his many blessings. The holiday recalls many memories.

I was nine years old. My brother and I played with our friends one brisk cold November afternoon. As the sun began to set, our friends went home to eat turkey, pumpkin pie and all the trimmings. My brother and I went home expecting the same. We sat down at the kitchen table waiting for a feast. My mother put five bowls of freshly made beans before my brothers and sisters as she said in a quivering voice in Spanish, "Give thanks to God for having something to eat." We understood. My father worked that day and couldn't eat with us.

There are many versions of how Thanksgiving Day originated. Throughout their history, the indigenous people on this continent observed some form of corn harvest celebration. Popular tales have American Indians inviting the Pilgrims to join in the celebration. The Indians had taught the Pilgrims many survival skills and shared their food after the disastrous winter of 1620-1621.

A favorite version is that the first Thanksgiving was a going-away party the Indians had thrown for the decimated Pilgrims, who were ready to go back. But after a bountiful harvest and a great party, they procrastinated and never left. That would be a nice version to believe.

William B. Newell, a Penobscot Indian and former chairman of the Anthropology Department of the University of Connecticut, offers another story: The first official Thanksgiving Day was celebrated by white settlers following their successful attack on an Indian settlement when the Indians were conducting religious ceremonies. According to Newell:

Thanksgiving Day was officially proclaimed by the governor of the Massachusetts Bay Colony in 1637 to commemorate the massacre of seven hundred men, women, and children who were celebrating their annual green corn dance in their own house.

Gathered in this meeting place they were attacked by mercenaries, English and Dutch. The Indians were ordered from the building and as they came forth they were shot down. The rest were burned alive in the building. The very next day, the governor declared a Thanksgiving Day. For the next hundred years, every Thanksgiving ordained by a governor was to honor a bloody victory, thanking God that the battle had been won.

I prefer my fond memories and wish that I had never learned that last version. Or maybe it is better that we do know. The taste such painful history leaves on a day like Thanksgiving is especially acrid. But for that too we can say, *Gracias.*

Or we can believe that the first Thanksgiving was celebrated on 30 April 1598 on the banks of the Río Grande, in the vicinity of what is now El Paso, Texas, years before the Pilgrims even landed on Plymouth Rock. On 20 April, 1598, Juan de Oñate's expedition arrived from Mexico City to the Conchos River. Tortured by thirst and exhaustion, the group rested and recuperated. Ten days later on the 30th, Ascension Thursday, they celebrated with a solemn high mass. Juan de Oñate naively took possession of the land in the name of His Catholic Majesty, Phillip II and called it the Kingdom of New Mexico. A Capitán Farfán wrote and presented a comedy, a theatrical piece he had authored. This became the first Euro-American play presented in the United States. Of particular interest was Juan de Oñate's wife who was the daughter of Don Hernan Cortés and the great-granddaughter of Moctezuma. Señora de Oñate, a descendant of the two great leaders who clashed and merged to create a new race of Mexicanos and Chicanos was not present but joined him later.

Or finally, we could believe that the first Thanksgiving was celebrated by the first indigenous people. Among the indigenous, Thanksgiving is not an annual celebration but a common everyday practice to request nourishment from Mother Earth and to give her thanks. You don't just take and give thanks afterword.

IN DEFENSE OF THE JALAPEÑO AND OTHER CHILES

A cartoon in the *New Yorker* shows a smiling Eskimo street vendor selling blubber in midtown Manhattan, while a wrapped up Euro American walks by in the snow. Humorous though it may be, the cartoon also carries a clear and loud message about the infusion of exotic third world foods not only on the streets of New York but throughout the country.

As salsa outsells ketchup and Taco Bell outsells McDonald's, the latest wave is the introduction of more authentic Mexican restaurants. A little too smug and comfortable with the growing availability of the real thing, we should have expected the competition to come up with something.

So it was no surprise that a recent small article in the *San Francisco Chronicle* was headlined "Hot Chili Peppers May Be Carcinogenic." The Cox News Service article stated that some "epidemiologists" from Yale University and the Mexico National Institute of Public Health "had concluded" that chili peppers "may be" carcinogenic, cancer producing. Laboratory experiments with animals and cells in test tubes had already found that capsaicin, the hot producing agent in the peppers, is a carcinogen.

Dr. Robert Dubrow, a Yale Medical School epidemiologist, studied the incidence and distribution of stomach cancer and the eating habits of 1,000 residents in Mexico City.

Mexico City? It's the biggest city on earth with more than twenty million souls and over twenty-five million projected by the year 2,000. With all the smog, congestion, and earthquakes that afflict its residents, why they didn't study people in rural areas or a more sedate and relaxed Mexican town, like Brownsville or some other town on the border is a convenient mystery. They didn't have to go to Mexico City, unless they were after particular findings.

According to their studies, heavy consumers of hot chili peppers were seventeen times more likely to have stomach cancer than those who never eat hot peppers at all. Even people who considered themselves "medium" eaters were four times more likely to have stomach cancer. But what role did smog, earthquakes and big city nerves have in causing this?

Of course the two most interesting words in the headline and the article are "may be." The article stated their conclusion that chili peppers "may be" carcinogenic. Are they or are they not? The conclusion is "Maybe!" They weren't sure but felt compelled to broadcast their iffy conclusion.

How or why (two important questions for journalists) this study was thought up and who funded it should also be newsworthy. According to the article, per capita consumption of chili peppers in this country more than doubled from 1982 to 1992. "Pace Picket Chile Sauce," made in Santone, is a big seller in Mexico. Was this funded by a McDonald's or was the Ketchup Association trying to catch up? And so how many readers will believe and begin to boycott jalapeños due to this inconclusive study while they continue to consume carcinogenic California table grapes?

Cesar Chavez had led a five-year boycott of California table grapes when he died. For years, the United Farm Workers have been sounding a warning about the danger of agricultural pesticides. Some 300,000 farm workers a year are stricken with pesticide-related illnesses. Childhood cancer and birth defects have reached epidemic proportions in many San Joaquin Valley towns. Yet you don't see Yale University epidemiologists coming to study this. You don't see the Mexican Institute for Public Health trying to protect their poor emigrant farm workers from the pesticides in this country. Not until the mainstream majority in this country begins to feel the effects will any study be done. Until then,

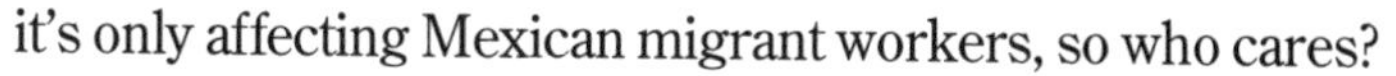

it's only affecting Mexican migrant workers, so who cares?

Meanwhile, a month after the inconclusive jalapeño scare, Florida legislators were trying to consider a bill that would give farmers the right to sue anyone who defames their crops. Criticize a cucumber, bad-mouth a bell pepper, insult a lettuce and you may have a day in court with possible jail time.

Under such a proposed law, farmers could slap a lawsuit on anyone who publicly states that a Florida-grown food product is unsafe for human consumption without reliable scientific facts to back up their claim.

A year before these two articles came out, there was a study out of Stanford University's Center for Research in Disease Prevention, which stated that the traditional diet of Mexican Americans is healthier than that of Euro Americans. That totally goes against the grain of what we have heard all our lives, but according to the study, Mexican Americans eat less cheese, fried foods, red meat and cured meat such as hot dogs, and add less fat to food after cooking. They also eat more healthy foods high in carbohydrates and fiber, such as rice, corn and dried beans.

According to the study, the more acculturated you become, the more you take on Euro American's bad habits. In July of 1994 yet another highly publicized study concluded that Mexican food is high in fat and cholesterol. The contradictions of these studies are confusing, but it appears that Americans can create Mexican fast foods that are less healthy by preparing beans cooked with lard, fried meats, and by adding an abundance of sour cream, guacamole, and cheeses. It seems untrue because this isn't really the authentic cuisine of Mexico. All these contradictory news items go to prove only one thing, with the right funding and an abiding press you can prove just about anything. Viva el jalapeño!

post script

Months after writing this, and a whole lifetime as a jalapeño consumer, aficionado, advocate and activist I was diagnosed with an abdominal tumor. (Pause for a last laugh, or you may want to read a more detailed account in the last essay of this collection.)

My alternatives here could have been to be obstinate on the unconvincing studies of 1,000 chile pepper eaters in Mexico City, a megapolis of 20 million. Natives of Veracruz, home of the Jalapeño, or people from the Northern state of Chihuahua who consume more hot peppers than Chilangos, Mexico City natives.

However, people will respectfully believe whatever they want to believe. Some friends pointed out that maybe it was the jalapeños that caused my tumor. Without dismissing that possibility, I'm also acutely aware of other probable causes. I even believe that Jalapeños have antioxidants that prevent cancer. However, "maybe" like radiation treatment for cancer, too much of a good thing or a bad thing can cause cancer.

I won't live my life observing all the "maybe" caution signs. So I will eat jalapeños again, but moderately and mildly. Besides, what kind of a Mexicano or Chicano would not love and defend jalapeños?

HOME BY THE SEA

From our two-story retreat home in Carmel Highlands, California, the west spans toward the vast and eternally sinking horizon of the Pacific Ocean. Most days the sky is as blue as the ocean. Below, white crests eternally ride atop the blue surf breaking and bathing the dark brown rocks of Point Lobos. Behind to the East, beautiful green Cypress trees rise against the hills and a few nestled homes. To the south along the Coast lies beautiful Big Sur country. To the North more beautiful coastlines, the Carmel Mission, San Carlos Borromeo del Río Carmelo.

This is California, California at its most beautiful. Less than 150 years after this territory was claimed by Mexicanos and Indians, a pervading and almost insistent indigenous ambiance persists. It is a ghostlike charm that lingers in the Carmel Mission, its Indian cemetery, historic Mexican and Spanish adobe architecture, Casa Pacheco, Casa Vasquez, the old Mexican jail, and names like Carmelo, Monterey, Alvarado and Big Sur.

Big Sur? As in "Big Sir" or "Big Surf?" "Big Sur" is an incomplete translation of what was once *El País Grande al Sur,* or more commonly called *la costa al sur.* Big Sur means Big South.

Carmel Highlands is an exclusive but not necessarily high income small town with a population of just under five hundred, just south of Carmel and along California's Pacific Coast Highway, once called *El Camino Real.*

Somehow, some way or another, with savings, searching for a good deal, an honest sales agent, and after a prior investment loss, my wife, Cecilia, and I borrowed on the equity of our home to purchase a modest, comfortable home overlooking the ocean.

Our dreams of living in such a setting had never gone beyond wishful thinking. Only a fortunate few live on the California coast. A block away from our home is the late Ansel Adams' home. The area is lightly populated and serene. The clear night skies are littered with stars. The coast has been officially designated as a National Wildlife Refuge. During February, the great whale migration can be appreciated from our windows. From a sandy beach cove two blocks away seals sun bathe on the rocks or play hide and seek in the water. It is beautiful beyond description. The Indians considered this area sacred.

I think of the beauty and our good fortune and remember a persistent suggestion from a dear departed friend, "Write about your new surroundings, as Chicanos." There is a tease that arouses my discomfort. A Chicano landowner! A capitalist! On prime California land! Probably the only Chicanos in Carmel Highlands or neighboring Carmel and one of a few on the entire California Coast.

Criticism or teases of Chicanos with fancy cars and homes not normally found in the barrios is prevalent. This criticism comes from Chicanos and Gringos alike who erroneously stereotype land-owning Chicanos as *vendidos,* sellouts, or Marxist socialists gone wrong.

I'm reminded of two unforgettable anecdotes. First was the young Chicana Stanford graduate who became a doctor. She confided how crushed she was to see me in a coat and tie at a University function. She had the naive but prevalent assumption that all Chicanos wore nothing but working-class clothes. Second was a student who asked to borrow my siphoning hose. When I informed him that I didn't have one he answered, "Oooohhh . . . What kind of a Chicano are you anyway?" Another time, the same *bato,* may he now rest in peace, asked if he could borrow my jumper cables. Again I didn't have any and again he responded, "Oooohhh . . . What kind of a Chicano are you anyway?"

Chicanos have forever been attacked for wearing a coat and tie, or for owning property because we are breaking new ground into formerly exclusive white territory. Once a Chicano in an audience asked Luis Valdez if he could still consider himself a Chicano with probable wealth and fame. His answer, "Do I have to be poor to be a Chicano?"

Our neighbors in Carmel Highlands are most gracious and accepting. From our home in Carmel Highlands, we appreciate and relate to the regional history and can readily identify and feel that somehow the land is returning to the people that once lived here. Not only returning to *Mexicanos,* but to *indígenas,* to Chicanos, half breeds with indigenous ancestors. Yankees have always justified stealing the land from Mexicanos because Mexicanos stole it from Indians without realizing that Mexicanos are more Indian than Hispanic. And so in the name of our indigenous ancestors, we reclaim the land, with deed and title, once we pay off the mortgage.

But we are not the only Mexicanos in the area. The surrounding fields of Monterey County produce eighty-five percent of the artichokes consumed in this country. You need not be told who the farmworkers are.

The poorest of our new neighbors live in shacks by the expensive artichoke fields. I visited these farmworkers one day wanting to give away a futon bed.

One dying afternoon as the orange sun was setting over the green artichoke fields and the blue ocean, I drove onto the brown dirt road by their paint-faded one room homes and in Spanish asked a farmworker if he could use the bed tied to the top of my van.

"¿Como sabía que necesitaba una cama?" How did I know he needed a bed, he asked as he broke into a wide smile and throwing up his hands as if he had hit the jackpot.

"It's not very soft," I apologized after we assembled the futon on the dirt ground in front of his crowded home and an artichoke field.

"¡Hombre!" he answered, *"Esta noche,* I will sleep like a king!"

We talked. He was from Oaxaca. I judged him to be a good person and so I asked, "We are looking for a good, honest and responsible person to clean and maintain our house when we are away."

"Mi cuñada!" he answered. Pointing North beyond a hill, he said, "My sister-in-law and her husband live over there. They would be perfect."

And perfect they were. We interviewed the young Oaxacan couple, checked their reference, agreed to their hourly fee and gave them a key to clean our house when we were away." They were with us for a year and a half before they realized they were working too much at too many jobs and barely had time to start a family.

In fine Carmel and Monterey restaurants Mexicanos cook, wash, serve and wait on tables. With memories of our immigrant parents ingrained, we take pride in identifying with them. We ask them what part of Mexico they are from only to confirm that most Mexican immigrants around Monterey and Carmel come from Oaxaca. These are questions we don't ask undocumented Australian, Canadian or European workers.

One famous Monterey resident was author Robert Louis

Stevenson, author of *Treasure Island,* who lived in Carmel Valley. In the late 1800s he was able to appreciate the indigenous population and lamented, *The Monterey of last year exists no longer. A huge hotel has sprung up in the desert by the railway. Invaluable toilettes figure along the beach and between live oaks; and Monterey is advertised in the newspapers, and posted in the waiting rooms at railway stations as a resort for wealth and fashions. Alas for the little town! It is not strong enough to resist the influence of the flaunting caravanserai, and the poor, quaint, penniless native gentlemen of Monterey must perish, like a lower race, before the millionaire vulgarians of the Big Bonanza.*

But Mexicanos never did die away. Some have always lived in the shadows, in the shacks, the shanties—and worked in the sun filled fields. Our parents were the immigrant farmworkers who pulled us away from the fields to the schools, away from hard labor and exploitation. We are not self made, we do not owe what we have to individualistic self made success but to the sweat, struggle and tears of our parents.

But somewhere, somehow, many Chicanos and non-Chicanos lost the message or became blind to the words of Emiliano Zapata, the great Mexicano hero, revolutionary, martyr and icon. Said he, *La tierra es del que la trabaja*—The earth belongs to those who work it.

Real power begins and ends with land ownership. We don't have to be migrants in our own land. Our roots are deep in the soil and in the history of this land we are reclaiming.

PACHUCOS AND THE TAXICAB BRIGADE

Thursday, June 3, 1943, was a warm inviting night for over 50,000 military servicemen stationed around the Los Angeles area. Weekends began on Thursdays and this particular Thursday was soon after payday.

That evening, a group of eleven sailors walked into the middle of a barrio along the 1700 block of North Main Street. According to their documented statement, they were attacked by a gang of young Mexicans. The sailors, who claimed they were outnumbered three to one, suffered minor cuts and bruises.

The incident was reported to a police station. There, some of the policemen formed a "vengeance squad" and set out to arrest the gang that had attacked the sailors. By the time they got to the scene there were no Mexicans or Mexican Americans. The police raid was a fiasco, and the only solution left was to report it to the newspapers, which in turn whipped up the community and the military against the Mexican population.

The next night, approximately two hundred sailors decided to take the law into their own hands hiring a fleet of twenty taxicabs and cruising down the center of town toward East L.A. The first victim of the "Taxicab Brigade" was a young Mexican "zoot suiter" who was left badly beaten and bleeding. The total tally for that night: two 17-year-olds, one 19-year-old and one 23-year-old, all left on pavements or sidewalks for the ambulances to pick up. The police were unable or refused to intercept the Taxicab Brigade. It was just another punitive military expedition.

On June 4, the L.A. newspapers took a rest from the war news to play up the "Zoot Suit War," named after the zoot suits worn by Mexican-American youths. The local press adopted a just and righteous attitude on the part of the servicemen. On the following day, hundreds of soldiers and sailors paraded through downtown L.A., warning zoot suiters to closet their drapes or suffer the consequences. L.A. police, shore patrol and military police did nothing, apparently because of the number of frenzied servicemen involved.

On June 7, civilians joined their military counterparts and mobbed restaurants, bars and theaters in search of not only Mexicans but also "Negroes," and Filipinos.

The following is one eye-witness account by Al Waxman, editor of the *Eastside Journal:* "Four boys came out of a pool hall wearing the zoot suits. Police ordered them into arrest cars. One refused . . . The police officer answered with three swift blows of the night-stick across the boy's head and he went down. As he lay sprawled, he was kicked in the face. Police had difficulty loading his body into the vehicle because he was one-legged and wore a wooden limb. . .

"At the next corner, a Mexican mother cried out, 'Don't take my boy, he did nothing. He's only fifteen years old . . .' She was struck across the jaw with a night-stick and almost dropped the two and a half year old baby that was clinging in her arms..."

Waxman witnessed several other incidents and pleaded with the local police station but they answered, "It is a matter for the military police." The Mexican community was in turmoil. Mothers, fathers, sisters, aunts, and uncles swarmed police stations looking for their lost children.

By June 8, the L.A. district attorney declared "the situation is getting entirely out of hand." The mayor, however, thought matters would eventually blow over and after a count of the Mexicans in jail, the chief of police thought the situation had cleared up.

But it was not over for the press. The *Los Angeles Times* stated the riots were having a "cleansing effect." A *Herald-Express* editorial said the riots "promise to rid the community of . . . those zoot suited miscreants." Meanwhile, the "miscreant" military operations spread to the suburbs. The Los Angeles City Council adopted a resolution making the wearing of zoot suits a misdemeanor.

Finally, on the heels of a Navy declaration that downtown L.A. was "out of bounds," and following the Mexican ambassador's formal inquiry to the U.S. secretary of state, and other expressions of international concern, the *Los Angeles Times* took a conciliatory and pious tone, disassociating any possibility of bigotry from the riots. At the same time, the*Times* went on the offensive, attacking defenders Carey McWilliams and Eleanor Roosevelt for stirring up racial discord.

Similar "zoot suit" disturbances were reported in San Diego on June 9; in Philadelphia on June 10; in Chicago on June 15; and in Evansville, Indiana, on June 27. Bigotry-based riots also occurred in Detroit, Harlem and Beaumont, Texas.

Relations with Mexicans and Mexican Americans had seemed warm and friendly up to that point. But those were only diplomatic relations. In 1941, a bracero program had been agreed upon and signed by the two countries allowing Mexican farm workers to work on this side, thus freeing U.S. fieldhands to work in defense industries or in the military. A month before the June 3 riots, Mexican soldiers had paraded through downtown Los Angeles in a Cinco de Mayo celebration. At the same time, Mexican and U.S. navys exchanged information on Japanese activities off the coast of Baja California.

The riots lasted for ten days, ending on June 13, 1943. Unlike modern riots, these were sporadic and scattered fights. No one was killed or sustained massive injuries. Property damages and convictions were minimal. And it was not the Mexican American youths who rioted but the military. Carey McWilliams, author of *North From Mexico,* called them "Government Riots."

In *The Zoot Suit Riots*, Mauricio Mazón, a history professor at the University of Southern California, wrote, "at least for ten days in Southern California . . . the military lost control of several thousand servicemen." Several archived military memos confirm the image of an impotent military brass. The frenzy was fed by the press, which predicted massive retaliations by Mexican zoot suiters.

There were no political manifestos or heroes originating from the riots—except for the "pachucos," the first Mexican American youths to rebel and strike their own self-identity through the zoot suit. To this day they live in literature, films, murals, dance and historical accounts. They live, too, through their social and cultural descendants, the *cholos.*

The pachuco has enjoyed a cultural aura, complete with stylistic pathos. He was both a tragic and heroic figure—a mythical creation. El Pachuco is the preeminent Don Quixote of Aztlán (the mythical southwest where the Aztecs began their journey to found Tenochtítlan, today's Mexico City).

This powerful figure has captured the imagination of artists, writers, poets and philosophers including Nobel prize winner Octavio Paz who in 1950 devoted the first chapter of

Labyrinth of Solitude, his classic study of the Mexicano character, to "El Pachuco and Other Extremes." Although Paz maligned the Pachuco, he now recants and regrets that early analysis. His chapter offered a derisive condemnation of not only an adolescent caught between adulthood and youth but also caught between two countries, two vastly different cultures. The carefree adolescent years enjoyed by Anglo-American youths of the '40s were nonexistent in Mexican culture. For Mexican youth, the age of fifteen became a rite of passage into adulthood, while young Mexican Americans chose to affirm a new identity.

A few years ago, Octavio Paz came to Stanford. At a dinner party my wife and I politely asked him for his views about Chicanos. *¡No sé!* he answered, refusing to touch the topic but attentive to our views.

Even before Paz's essay, Chilean author and Stanford University Emeritus Professor Fernando Alegría wrote the first known short story on El Pachuco in 1945, "Al Otro Lado De La Cortina."

José Montoya, a Chicano multidisciplinary artist, poet, muralist, musician, founder and general of Sacramento's RCAF (Royal Chicano Air Force, earlier known as the Rebel Chicano Art Front) has concentrated many of his poetic, musical and artistic works on El Pachuco. He lived the pachuco era, and his poem "El Louie" is a classic Chicano poem.

Luis Valdez's award-winning play and film *Zoot Suit* was the national debut for Edward James Olmos, who played the character of El Pachuco and whose black, zoot-suited image on posters elevated the zoot suit to the realm of an icon. Olmos then wrote, directed and starred in the film *American Me,* which captures the Zoot Suit riots of 1943 and follows the pachuco's descendants right down to the present day cholos. The tragedy of urban Mexican-American youth has also been explored in *Stand and Deliver*, and most recently *Bound by Honor.*

Within this cultural aura, lies an important linguistic mystery: the origin of the term "pachuco." McWilliams suggests that the term came from Mexico and denoted resemblance to the gaily costumed people living in the town of Pachuca. He further suggests that it was first applied to border bandits in the vicinity of El Paso. Although McWilliams believes that the pachuco stereotype was born in L.A., it was El Paso, Texas, better known as EPT or El Chuco that had the reputation for the "meanest" pachucos.

Another little known theory is offered by 79-year-old San José State University Emeritus Professor Jorge Acevedo. As a conscientious objector, Acevedo resisted induction into WWII. For this action, he was sentenced to San Quentin but soon released to do community work as a counselor for braceros and homosexuals. Acevedo's theory is that the pachucos grew out of the repatriation program when more than 350,000 Mexicanos and Mexican Americans (the unofficial count among some historians is double that number), were deported to Mexico by the government during the Depression.

Acevedo recalls working through churches and social organizations to smuggle U.S. citizens of Mexican descent back to their homes in this country. He remembers *el barrio* Belvedere in East Los Angeles being emptied overnight. "They came at five in the morning with trucks and buses to drive them to Tijuana. Through a desire for vengeance and revenge, pachucos came from this experience." Pachucas were equals with their male peers because of equal victimization and codependency.

Most history books in this country are silent on this subject. To combat this vacuum of history, Stanford University Chicano students at Casa Zapata, the Chicano Theme residence, annually celebrate Zoot Suit Month. For one month each year, talks, lectures, films, discussions, and workshops on the zoot suit, dress styles, hairdos, dancing and music of that era are presented.

In a recent panel discussion entitled "El Pachuco: the Myth, the Legend and the Reality," Fernando Soriano, a visiting psychology professor at Stanford, presented a study on contemporary Chicano gangs. He noted the lack of real role models for Chicano youth and how the figure of the pachuco fills the gap by offering a role model and a sense of rebellion against society, an opportunity to gain respect even if negative.

Professor Soriano noted the significant increases in gang activities and the growing number of female Chicanas in gangs. From 452 gang-related homicides in 1988, the number jumped to 700 homicides in 1992 in L.A. He questioned what gangs and homicides have to do with pachucos.

Fast to respond, José Montoya declared, "Gangs and homicides have nothing to do with pachucos. The drug lords dumped this shit on our barrios and we are stuck with it. The cartel brought in the drugs, firepower and finances to move kids away from the fast food franchises." He went on to advise, "We need to lay down our fears about glamorizing the pachuco and showcase the important and viable aspects of the Chicano experience. As offspring of Mexican and Mexican-American parents we need to see what it was like growing up . . ."

"Working-class servicemen from other parts of the country came thinking the L.A. barrios were exotic ports of entry. Seeing Chicanos for the first time freaked them out. Industrialists, such as newspaper mogul William Randolph Hearst were already angry with Mexican President Cárdenas's nationalization of the oil industry. This wartime hysteria was translated for the Spanish lanzguage media, such as *La Opinión*. This didn't help Mexican and Mexican-American parents understand their children's rebellion."

Montoya calls the historical silence on these roundups shameful for this country, ". . . but they shouldn't be for us. This is something that was put upon us at the same time Chicano soldiers were disproportionately winning more Congressional Medals of Honor than any other group. Pachucos were not all gangsters or *batos locos*. Some came from the fields and dressed up on weekends."

The third panel member, Renato Rosaldo, Professor of Social Anthropology at Stanford and author of *Culture and Truth* agreed with Montoya.

Rosaldo noted the pachuco's exaggeration of the social norm, "putting it in your face . . . The pachuco exaggeration is a way of producing cultural resistance, a cultural style to modify the existing norm with little or no Mexican symbolism. There is a kind of reversal resistance," he added, "the slow and low of a lowrider when the opposite American ethic is fast and efficient. Nothing is so infuriating as a car that's going very slow and low. Worse than speeding."

Rosaldo noted the dress styles and how the body goes beyond the clothes to become part of the style. Instead of leaning slightly forward, slouch shouldered like business men, the Pachucos leaned back, shoulders thrown back and with long hand gestures. There is a Mexicaness in the formality along with self dramatization and theatricality. Whereas the Anglo-American norm tends to be spontaneous, "be yourself," and informal, without spelling it out or being conscious.

In *American Me* Rosaldo saw very little heroism left in the heroic figure, finding instead a devastating criticism of a version of masculinity where there is no alternative. Olmos seemed to be crying out, "Stop the war! Wherever this stuff is coming from it's destroying us!"

Rosaldo also believes it is demeaning to us to believe that a style of dress is responsible for the present day tragedies. A good example is the zoot suit style of dress. The origin of the zoot suit has been traced to New York and Detroit, but it goes further back to Europe. In an interview with Chuy Varela of Berkeley, California, renowned musician Cab Calloway traced the Zoot Suit to England. In the thirties, according to Calloway, the British clothing industry manufactured thousands of zoot suits as the latest style which would take hold. It didn't catch on and so they were dumped on the U.S. Market. When they reached New York, and Harlem in particular, African Americans took to them with pleasure and satisfaction. From New York's Harlem they were passed on to Detroit and Chicago. Those were the direct lines of migration for African Americans. For the Mexican-American urban migrants it was El Paso, Chicago, Detroit and Los Angeles. African American ghettoes, jobs, modest modes of transportation, music and styles of dress greatly attracted Mexican Americans.

The comparisons between yesterday's pachucos and today's cholos are fascinating. Psychohistorian and USC Professor Mauricio Mazón authored the book *The Zoot-Suit Riots: The Psychology of Symbolic Annihilation.* During and after the riots, Mexican-American youth were known to have shaved their heads, "a kind of scarification that indicated their victimization by servicemen." Fifty years later, some cholos tattoo a black tear below one of their eyes as a mark of incarceration.

Cholos are cultural descendants of the pachucos. A *cholo* is defined as a *mestizo* of Indian and European blood, in most Spanish dictionaries. A secondary definition is tinged with old world bigotry as it defines a cholo as a "civilized Indian." The term came to this country through the many Peruvians who arrived here during the California Gold Rush. It was used to describe Indians living along the Peruvian Coast. In California the Peruvians called poor mestizos *cholos.*

Closely related to the word cholo is the term *bato.* Pancho Villa's revolutionary army was made of *batos vagos,* vagrant friends. *Batos vagos* has further evolved into the caló slang as *bato locos,* crazy dudes. The slang, called caló but better known as Spanglish or Mex-Tex, has been utilized by the pachuco and the cholo both. Caló was originally *zincaló,* the idiom of Spanish gypsies. Interestingly enough, *calcos* is the same word pachucos, cholos and gypsies use for shoes.

In Mexico, the pachuco was seen as the Anglo-Americanization of a Mexicano or, according to Paz, an extremity of what a Mexicano can become. In Mexico pachucos were called Tarzanes, perhaps because pachucos had long hair like Tarzan in the popular movies. Through Mexican comedian and film actor Germán Valdés, popularly known as "Tin Tan," the pachuco became a novelty in Mexico.

Tin Tan has to be credited with taking Mexican-American influences to Mexico in the form of dress styles, music, calo and english words. Germán Valdez was the son of a mexican consul who took his family to live in Laredo, El Paso and Los Angeles. When Tin Tan was young he befriended Mexican-American pachucos, took their music and style, introducing it with humor on Mexico City stages and theater. He made over one hundred films and became a legend. In Juarez, Mexico, a zoot-suited Tin Tan sculpture looks over the old *Mercado.*

The pachuco was also called a *tirilongo* and though the word's origin is vague pachucologist José Montoya believes it might have been related to pachucos declaring their citizenship at the bridge. Instead of declaring U.S. Citizen, they blurted, "tirilongo." *Tirilón* also meant long threads, thus

Tirilongo was a blend of the english and spanish. But a *tirilona* was not a pachuca, she was an informant.

Social anthropologist José Cuellar, alias musician Doctor Loco, further sees the pachuco as one of the first precursors to multiculturalism, without the pachuco knowing what the word meant. In style, language, dress but especially in music, the pachuco borrowed from the Anglo-American, the African American, the Mexicano and the Caribbean to create a new and different kind of music. We now call it transculturalism.

In the end, the pachuco was the precursor of the Chicanos and the Chicano Movement. The pachucos were the first Mexican Americans to rebel against this country and their mother country, the first to stake their own universal identity and independence from both oppressive cultures, to mold their own, a renaissance-hybrid of both.

Beyond the zoot suit riots are the unmistakable spiritual cries of aesthetic expression through pachucos, cholos, zoot suiters, low riders, murals, language, cholos. Through Chicano theater, film, literature and art, there is an assertion, a cultural and aesthetic identity that today takes its place as part of the American experience.

THE HONORABLE SENATOR RALPH W. YARBOROUGH

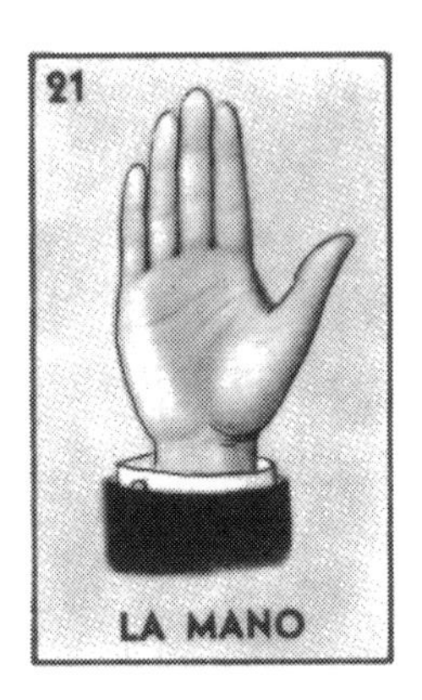

Writers always remember the first time their work is published. The thrill of seeing one's own printed name beneath the title of an essay, poem or story is unforgettable. Quite by chance, my first publication was in the U.S. Congressional Record for September 2, 1964, although I didn't find out about it until a year later.

In 1964 after four years in the military I continued my studies at Texas Western College, now the University of Texas at El Paso, but it was difficult. In those days there was no financial assistance for minorities or Cold War veterans. I had heard about Texas Senator Ralph W. Yarborough's proposal for a Cold War G.I. Bill. Since the Korean War, millions of military servicemen had served in the Cold War without benefits.

So I wrote Texas Senator Ralph W. Yarborough, a Democrat and populist of the first order:

El Paso, Texas
August 19, 1964

Dear Senator Yarborough: I am writing you in reference to the proposed cold War G.I. bill which you introduced. My deep interest in this bill is shared by thousands of other young men for the following reasons:

I am now 23 years of age and have just completed a four-year tour of duty with the U.S. Air Force.

Since my return to civilian life I have found myself in a precarious situation. My future is not very bright without a college education. I consider myself young and ambitious but cannot afford to continue my education without help. I have not been able to find a suitable full-time or part-time job. Many ex-servicemen have returned home and found nothing awaiting them. Such is the position I find myself in. Unless this new G.I. bill is soon passed a lot of us will have to settle for second-rate jobs and no education.

In the near future the draft will be eliminated. Thus a new generation of young men will not be obliged to serve, nor will they have to live through years of uncertainty waiting to be drafted, not knowing what course to take. At such a young age men should be forming and shaping their lives.

The Cold War has produced innumerable tensions, anxieties, and hazards upon today's servicemen. They have played the greatest role in the development of what the United States is so rightly proud of—guarding the peace and maintaining the strongest power on earth. Vietnam, Guantánamo, Berlin, Korea, Panama, Turkey and hundreds of other unheard of and isolated places are the homes of the servicemen. Some die in Vietnam, others suffer hardships, and quite a few are separated from their loved ones. The soldier, sailor and airman are quite underrated in this country and sometimes taken for granted.

The last two military pay raises should not be considered as a benefit to the military. That is to say that such a raise was approved basically because of the previous low wages.

For these reasons I urge you to expedite this bill, not only for my personal benefit but for my former comrades in arms and the nation. Further, I would deeply appreciate it if you could advise me of its present and future status.

José Antonio Burciaga
Airman First Class, U.S. Air Force Inactive Reserve

The good Senator Yarborough liked the letter enough to take it to the Senate Floor one day, read it aloud and requested that it be published in *The Congressional Record.* There being no objection, my letter was published.

But it was not until a year later that I found out. In 1965 I took a summer trip to Washington D.C. looking for work. In D.C. I had a friend, Tom Dunigan, who worked as a college intern at Senator Yarborough's office. I mentioned the Cold War G.I. Bill and he handed me a green covered government book on the Cold War G.I. Bill Hearings. I reached for the book and began leafing through the pages until my name jumped out at me. I couldn't believe it; there it was, published in the distinguished and historical Congressional Record, thus giving me some form of immortality.

The Cold War G.I. Bill was passed in 1966 and I was able to reap its educational fruits for three years of college, and a year of study at The San Francisco Art Institute.

I never forgot the good senator and briefly shook his hand one time in the Nation's capitol. But the Cold War G.I. Bill was not the sole reason for my admiration for this man. In Texas, a state with a notoriously racist history against Mexicanos, Ralph W. Yarborough was championing their causes. It was amazing, long before the Chicano Movement, this man was helping. Besides the Cold War G.I. Bill, the senator also introduced two other major pieces of legislation that had great significance and beneficial impacts on Latinos everywhere: one was the Bilingual Education Act and the second was the Minimum Wage Law.

On a 1991 trip to the University of Texas at Austin I arranged for a one hour interview with the Senator at his home through Marta Cotera, a friend and long-time activist. I not only wanted to thank him for starting me off on my writing career and for the G.I. Bill, but I was also curious about his life long commitment to helping the Mexican-American community in Texas when it was not popular, long before any Anglo politician found it politically safe.

So it was one Friday afternoon in November of 1991 that I rang the doorbell to the very charming but unpretentious Yarborough home in an upper middle-class Austin neighborhood. The Senator himself opened the door and momentarily startled me. Despite his eighty-eight years I hardly noticed a wrinkle on his face and his long silver hair gave him a more liberal appearance than I had imagined.

With a firm handshake he invited me in, introduced me to his wife Opal and led me into his beautifully furnished living room. The Senator walked slowly as he apologized for a bad back and wearing a brace. He sat in a straight chair with arm rests and next to him was a small table piled with a few books, pamphlets and papers pertaining to his Senate career. I wanted to delve into a more personal side of him, his early life and association with the Mexican-American community. But the Senator was prepared with his own agenda and out of respect, I listened to his fascinating stories of struggles, victories and defeats. His voice was soft and twanged with an East Texas accent. A recorder helped me double check his words.

"One of my greatest victories was the passage of the Cold War G.I. Bill," the Senator said, "despite opposition by President Eisenhower, President Kennedy, it finally passed through President Johnson in 1966." Basic opposition had come from the Pentagon but Senator Yarborough had kept the bill alive in every session. "It passed," he claims, "because the war in Vietnam got so unpopular President Johnson couldn't hold the tide any longer."

By the mid 1970's more than 8,200,000 veterans had been affected by the Cold War G.I. Bill. It covered widows of soldiers killed in combat and enabled wives of permanently disabled veterans and their children to get an education. Its benefits were not only for education but also for agriculture, home buying and building. Like the former G.I. Bills, the country reaped its investment through a greater tax base from educated and home owner veterans. That bill, he claims, "was the longest, hardest fight of my senatorial career."

In 1994, the first G.I. bill, for World War II veterans, celebrated its 50th anniversary. More than a benefit, these G.I. Bills were a just compensation for the service of individuals who had not been able to afford college. To this day the country has reaped greatly through the higher income and property taxes these veterans paid.

Seating next to a pile of books and pamphlets, Senator Yarborough handed me a monograph listing his accomplishments. In 1991, Senator Yarborough was honored with a Humanitarian Award by the Texas Democratic Women for ". . . his many significant contributions to the cause of human rights by legislation while serving in the United States Senate." In twelve years, Senator Ralph Yarborough had accomplished more than most legislators hope to in a lifetime. The few bills mentioned here are but milestones in a long list of other legislation he helped pass.

Of significant focus in this award was his 1966 Minimum Wage Increase and Expansion Bill. "For the first time, the minimum wage was extended to employees in retailing, laundries, restaurants, hotels, hospitals and agricultural workers. It was called theWidows amendment because it covered so many low-paying jobs which women usually held."

He helped co-sponsor the Higher Education Act of 1965 to assist qualified high school graduates to attend college through scholarships, graduate fellowships, low interest loans to students and work-study programs.

In 1966 he also introduced the first Bilingual Education Bill that became law. This legislation grew out of several education conferences in the Southwest that focused attention on the language learning barrier affecting over 1.7 million Spanish-speaking children.

"I not only attended meetings and studied the problem of Spanish-speaking children, but I had seen the language barriers and resulting poverty first hand."

In 1919 he graduated from Tyler High School and received an appointment to the U.S. Military Academy at West Point. After one year, he had firmly decided that a career in the Army was not what he wanted. At seventeen, Yarborough taught in one-room schools around his hometown and continued his college education at Sam Houston State College in Huntsville. At eighteen he was ready to see the world and worked his way across the Atlantic on a cattle-boat from New Orleans, wound up in Berlin, hired as Assistant Secretary of the American Chamber of Commerce, learned German and entered the Stendhal Academy. By 1923 he was back in Texas to enroll at the University of Texas Law School. In 1927 he graduated with highest honors and set out to distinguish himself as a recognized authority in land and water rights law. At the University of Texas Law School he lectured on land law.

Senator Yarborough explained, "In 1927, as a fresh law graduate from the University of Texas at Austin I joined a large El Paso law firm representing corporations, not people. Nonetheless, being a people-oriented young man I came to know and love the Mexican and Mexican-American people." On Saturdays and Sundays Mr. Yarborough would cross the border to Juarez to enjoy a good dinner. "When you could catch quail along the Río Grande," he recalled.

In 1928, the young attorney married his childhood sweetheart, Opal Warren, and brought her to El Paso. She became ill and for awhile needed the daily care and help of two Mexican women. "They were just wonderful, taking care of my wife." When Opal got well, the Yarboroughs decided to register in a Spanish class, two nights a week, at a local high school. This lasted two months before he was offered the position of Assistant Attorney General of Texas. "That ended my chance to learn conversational Spanish. Had it not been for that offer I would've stayed in El Paso and learned Spanish. But my real interest was aroused during my four years as Assistant Attorney General, that was when I became became acquainted with the Mexican-American educational problems." Following his tenure as Assistant Attorney General, he was appointed a District Judge for five years and those educational problems became even more apparent.

By 1938 Ralph Webster Yarborough had established a

distinguished background that included an East Texas political heritage, a region well known for its populist politicians. Yarborough became the most prominent.

How he got into politics is almost due to the generous permission of his future wife Opal who warned him about running for County Attorney in his native Henderson County. "If you run, the wedding is off. I won't marry a man in politics." Ralph loved her enough to set his ambitions aside and joined the El Paso law firm. By 1938, Opal had changed her mind and found no objection to Yarborough running for Texas Attorney General on a shoestring budget and using the old family car. "In that year driving through West Texas and seeing the migratory laborers and children pulling the cotton sacks, I first saw the terrible shape they were in and the few rights they had. I decided then that if the opportunity ever came I would do something about that."

He lost that first campaign but his taste for public life had set in so well that it survived through six unsuccessful statewide campaigns for Governor and Senator. Or as he puts it, "I ran for statewide office nine times: Won three, lost three and had three stolen from me. Texas percentages."

It was through these campaigns that Ralph Yarborough refined his populist method of meeting people on a personal basis, the handshake and look in the eye. He totally mistrusts the modern media hype of managed public relations with pseudo-images of candidates.

With the Pearl Harbor attack in 1941 he volunteered for

the Army as a Captain and served as a Judge Advocate at the Pentagon before requesting combat service. He served with the 97th Division under General George Patton's Third Army and saw action in the drive to liberate Czechoslovakia. After the war, Lt. Colonel Yarborough continued his military service under General Douglas MacArthur's command as a military government officer in Japan.

His return to Texas after World War II provided new opportunities with a background bound to impress any voter. But Texas politics is a whole different animal in the U.S. political arena. Just the names of some of the populist characters that have risen from that state are fascinating: "Cactus Jack" Garner served two terms as Vice President of the United States under President Franklin D. Roosevelt and was a former Speaker of the House.There was "Pa" and "Ma" Ferguson, "Pappy" O'Daniel, and of course, Lyndon Baines Johnson, to name a few.

Yarborough lost Texas political races in '52, '54 and '56 which included a volley of mudslinging and character assassinations during Senator McCarthy's era. But Senator Yarborough never gave in to personal slander. When asked if he and President Lyndon Baines Johnson were ever at odds he answers no. "Sometimes he said some things about me but I didn't answer or pay any attention because we both had people back home who supported the both of us."

His opportunity to serve in the U.S. Senate came as a result of a special Texas election called for when the seat was made vacant by the November election of Price Daniel as Governor. Once in the Senate, Lyndon Johnson and Ralph

Yarborough became a formidable pair, but oftentimes it was Johnson who stole the limelight as Senate Majority Leader and later as Vice President and President.

Nonetheless, Senator Yarborough gives much credit to Johnson for his accomplishments. When Johnson was Senate Majority Leader he helped select Yarborough for the Senate Labor and Public Welfare Committee. A senator on the Labor and Public Welfare Committee died and it became very controversial decision as to who would inherit that position. Liberals wanted Senator Joseph Clark, an outstanding liberal from Pennsylvania and the Conservatives wanted Senator Strom Thurmond, who was a Democrat at that time. Senator Yarborough recalls, "Lyndon didn't want to offend either side, so he said, 'Well, I got somebody from my native state I need to show a favor'." Senator Yarborough's entrance into the committee was unopposed after he promised both sides he wasn't necessarily a liberal or a conservative. "I didn't want to get beat before I started." No one knew how this fresh young senator was going to vote. Soon after that, he was able to get on the Education Subcommittee, which is what he was really aiming for. As a former one-room school teacher, his priority was education.

A national health care plan is nothing new. Senator Yarborough advocated it back in the sixties. He tried to make it a national goal when he said, "I want to tackle what I believe to be the biggest domestic problem in this country today." Close to thirty years later the problem is even more critical.

Senator Yarborough was one of the last of the great populist *políticos* from the South. While Governor Bill Clinton's populist approach to his presidential campaign was commendable, it is mild compared to populists of twenty plus years ago.

Because of the bills he helped pass, employers who now had to pay fair "minimum wages" raised the necessary opposition to oust him in 1970. Senator Yarborough lost re-election. He had been able to unify Texas' fiercely independent progressive elements through the force of his personality and vigorous leadership. But there were people who didn't want to pay for what they called "the big spending ways." Nonetheless, Yarborough's legacy as a people's politician is secure.

I asked him which state, Texas or California, was more progressive for Mexican Americans. He responded by recalling a march he had made with Cesar Chavez and farmworkers in California's Central Valley, "...I've never seen farmers look as mad. The look of hate from the deputy sheriffs and special constables... I think the only reason they didn't shoot at us is because we had some senators with us, Fritz Mondale and Ted Kennedy... I just got a little smell of that..."

"What Mexican American stands out that you admire the most as a hero?"

"That would have to be Dr. Hector García of Corpus Christi. You know he did so much and founded the G.I. Forum."

Senator Yarborough was unspoiled by big business. In a

1958 Senatorial Campaign, the ultra-conservative *Dallas Morning News* accused Yarborough of receiving some $25,000 in campaign contributions from labor unions. Yarborough's opponents gleefully thought this would be the "kiss of death." This was the trump card at the crucial moment of the campaign. Yarborough came back with a correction. The Dallas paper had actually understated the amount of labor's contributions to his campaign. Yarborough pointed out that his opponent, Bill Blakely, was a well-known millionaire and so he appealed for even more campaign contributions from the "little people" for whom he was fighting. This dramatic political turnaround confounded his opponents and helped produce a grand victory. For the next five years, he became a strong supporter of the progressive Kennedy-Johnson program.

The Senator won't delve into old campaign wounds. Perhaps out of pain, or letting them be. It is well-known that President John F. Kennedy's fatal trip to Texas was to help heal the political factions in that state.

As I prepared to leave, the Senator acknowledged the love and support he had received from his wife Opal of sixty-three years. She was close by, gracious but also aware of her husband's frail condition at that moment.

Will we ever see a Senator like Yarborough from Texas or any other state? He was a true populist, who cared and voted for all people, but especially for the downtrodden.

¡AY CARAMBA!

C*aramba! Arriba! Arriba!* Speedy Gonzalez screams in a high pitched voice as he slips, slides and runs from one cartoon escapade to another. When Donald Duck travels South of the Border he expresses his frustration with a *¡Caramba!* In Berkeley, California, there is a Mexican restaurant named *Ay Caramba!* Harmless enough, caramba is an interjection used to express surprise, amazement or a little anger. It can be as mild as saying "Goodness!" or "Good Heavens!"

But caramba is a synonym for the root word *carajo* and in the supposed bible of the Royal Academy of the Spanish language, *El Diccionario de la Real Academia Española,* a carajo is a penis, "the virile member of the male," and what Speedy Gonzalez is really saying is "Penis! Up! Up!" And, the restaurant name translates to "Oh, Penis!"

Another synonym for carajo is *caray!* Caray and caramba are mildly disguised synonyms for the word *carajo,* which has many rich and varied meanings. But *El Diccionario de la Real Academia Española* claims only this definition for *carajo:* "The virile member of the male. A bad sounding interjection."

In a short story I used the word *carajo*. The story was selected for a high school literature anthology, but not before receiving a letter from the permissions editor who wanted to censor *carajo.* "Some teachers objected to it," she wrote. Instead of *carajo* could they use the word *idiota?* How they substituted *idiota* from *carajo* was a mystery until I discovered it was just one of many definitions for *carajo.*

Few Latinos, except for the authors of the Royal Dictionary, call their penis a *carajo.* Like most other *español* speaking folk, my use of *¡Carajo!* was to express amazement and surprise. Like so many other people that use *¡carajo! ¡caray !* and *¡caramba!.*

No! I wrote back to the Permissions Editor. You may not change *¡carajo!* to *¡idiota!* I explained and gave her an alternative: "If you do not want to use carajo, you may substitute *caray* for *carajo.* But not *¡caramba! ¡Caramba!* is too much like "Gee whiz!" That's why Speedy Gonzalez and Donald Duck use it.

Carajo also means tricky, mischievous, difficult and hard to resolve. Of course, a carajo is all those things but few Latinos ever make that relationship. The synonyms are endless, from *caracho, caray, carraspirina* to *baramba, baray,* and *carajo.*

The sometimes ignorant power of the Royal Academy of the Spanish Language angered if not amazed many Latin American writers because the word *carajo* was forbidden from the *Diccionario de la Real Academia* until the 1987 edition.

In *el Diccionario de Mejicanismos,* Francisco J. Sanatamaría assailed the powerful Royal Academy for not permitting the word carajo a definition in the dictionary, "...that 'sublime interjection,' the most expressive in our language. And what are the reasons for its dismissal? Because it is a vulgar word, some say. Disgraceful the language that only has words for the tame and the ladies . . . A language should be a palette where all social classes, ignorant or distinguished, may find a color to their satisfaction in order to express their ideas and passions, giving life and color to all concepts."

The etymology of the word carajo is old and thus long and complex, and uncertain. In his *Diccionario Secreto,* Camilo José Cela notes the word could have come from the Latin vulgate *characulus* that gave birth to *caraculum, carere* to copulate. That characulus could have originally come from the Greek *Xapáxlov.* Cela gives many possible origins to the word including the observation that carajo has *cara,* face and *ajo,* garlic and how one poet used *cara de ajo*, to suggest a penis. In Spain, *hechar ajos*—to throw garlic, is a pun that translates to throwing carajos. Carajo is also used to invalidate worth, *no vale un carajo*—it's not worth a carajo. To send someone al carajo, is to send him or her to a distant place, such as hell. The Secret Dictionary quotes various ancient erotic poems that utilize carajo as a phallic symbol.

According to this clandestine dictionary, even the word cariño, one of the most beautiful spanish words that translates to affection and love originally came from carajo.

In Mexico and the U.S., *¡carajo!* is a mild interjection when compared to the awe-mighty Mexican word *"chingado."* And, *chingado* has its own mildly disguised synonyms such as *"¡Chihuahua!"* or *chinelas.*

Though "chingado" is considered a vulgar word, it can be used ad infinitum, in a variety of ways, positively or negatively, from the basic *chingón* to *chingonométrico* depending on the context and intonation. But that's a whole other word and there is a whole book on that one word, entitled *El Chingolés.* ¡Caramba!

"LA MARGARITA" AND THE MANY STORIES OF MUJERES NAMED "MARGARITA"

At last count, there were over six people who claimed to be inventors of *La Margarita,* the all time, most popular mixed drink in the whole *mundo.* I thought it was my Tío Pancho who invented La Margarita . . . and still do. Yet I will respect the other claims because they make for fascinating reading, and involve women named Margarita.

Daniel Negrete, may he rest in peace, passed away at the age of 92 to the big Margarita in the sky. He claimed an official government paper in Mexico City authenticated his invention of la Margarita, though the anonymous official government paper has never been identified.

In 1936 Daniel Negrete managed the Garcí Crespo, a well known hotel in Puebla, Mexico. He had a *novia* who, naturally, was named Margarita. She had the salty habit of adding salt to whatever she drank. Thus Daniel was inspired to create a drink for her so that she wouldn't have to reach for the bowl of salt. Then he decided to mix tequila and Cointreau, an orange liqueur, and lime juice. Last he shook the ingredients with ice.

Around 1955, Vern Underwood, a California liquor distributor from Los Angeles, claims to have discovered where the Margarita was invented when he took note of an L.A. restaurant named The Tail of the Cock with unusually large orders of tequila. An unidentified bartender at The Tail was making Margaritas like tamales, one right after the other.

Vern discovered that a lovely Hollywood movie star was inviting everyone to try the bartender's new drink. In this case, no one knows or remembers the mystery woman or how it was baptized "Margarita." Nonetheless, this led to full-page advertisements with a picture of Vern saluting the goddess of tequila, La Margarita. Vern Underwood also claims to have brought the first bottle of José Cuervo into the United States in 1942. Considering the thousands of Mexicanos on both sides of the border for centuries, it is hard to believe that Vern Underwood was the first to bring a bottle of José Cuervo into this country. Smuggling Mexican liquor across the border has been as common as paying the bridge toll.

Next is a woman identified only as Doña Berta, who dates the Margarita circa 1930. According to Sara Morales, a Mexican folklore expert, Doña Berta was owner and bartender of Bertita's Bar in Taxco, Mexico. Berta already had a namesake drink called "Berta" when she created the Margarita. Salt on the glass was a Berta trademark.

Another woman named Margarita Sames from "Santone," Texas, claims to be the inventor of La Margarita. She even said so on the nationally televised *Good Morning America* show in the Spring of 1994. Her story starts in 1938 when *la muy simpática* Margarita Sames began visiting Acapulco, where she and her rancher-husband had a house near the Flamingo Hotel. She was known for her parties and Margarita just loved tequila and supposedly "drank it all day long." For Christmas of 1948, Margarita Sames combined it with Cointreau and lime and then served it in a cocktail glass. Thus was born the Margarita.

Then there's Carlos Herrera of San Diego who passed away in May of 1992 at the ripe age of ninety. He lived in Tijuana for many years and opened a restaurant called Rancho La Gloria, perhaps named after his daughter Gloria Amezcua.

In 1938 or 1939, according to Señor Herrera, he decided to mix a jigger of white tequila with lemon juice, shaved ice, triple sec and topped it off with salt. Local lore has it that one of his customers was a showgirl and sometime actress, who called herself Marjorie King. Because she was allergic to all hard liquor except tequila, which she didn't like to drink straight, Carlos decided to experiment and named the result Margarita, of course.

Next, enter Larry Cano, the originator of the El Torito chain of Mexican restaurants. He claims that in 1954 he was the first to take the basic ingredients and whirl them in a blender to make the "spiked icy popsicle" drink today known as the frozen Margarita.

Across Tijuana is also the Caliente Race Track, where they claim it surfaced around 1930.

Who to believe, who to believe? I grew up with my own story of La Margarita even before I was old enough to drink them because it was a family story. So mark your place and mix yourself a Margarita before reading on (skip the tequila if you are under age or refraining from alcohol due to medication or because it just makes you plain loco . . .):

On my Mother's side of the familia, there was a taboo against La Margarita. No one mentioned it and much less drank it in front of my Tía Bibi in Juarez or El Paso. My Tía Bibi was married to Francisco Morales, who we called Tío Pancho.

In 1942 the United States had entered World War II and Fort Bliss, the army base in El Paso, became a strategic training center. At the same time, Ciudad Juarez became the foreign port of call for thousands of G.I.s who sought fun and frolic on the famous Avenida Juarez strip.

This is where Tío Pancho comes in. He was a celebrated *cantinero* along the strip at a classy lounge named

Tommy's Place where he worked for 21 years. Some of his bartending colleagues, all union paying bartenders, still remember him as one of the best bartenders in Mexico. His renown was such that he was flown to bartend at private parties in the States.

In 1979 he recounted the story to Ron Arias, now a Senior Writer for *People* magazine:

"Fourth of July 1942," he recalled. "It's so vivid in my mind. A lady came in to Tommy's Place there in Juarez one afternoon and asked for a Magnolia. It was a popular ladies' drink in those days, but I forgot what it contained. I knew it had Cointreau, lime and ice, but couldn't remember what kind of liquor. So I used tequila.

" 'This isn't a Magnolia but it's very good,' she told me. 'What is it called?' There was already a drink named the Texas Daisy, so I thought the translation for daisy would be appropriate. Out of professional pride and being a Mexicano, I answered, 'Oh, I'm sorry. I thought you had asked for a Margarita.' " And so the Margarita was born.

This first Margarita was served from a shaker into a 6 ounce champagne class. It was not filled to the brim. This is in very bad taste, my Tío says.

The ingredients for the first Margarita were 4/5ths tequila, 1/5 Cointreau, half a lime and large pieces of chipped ice. Because it was too strong, it was soon modified to 2/3 tequila, 1/3 Cointreau, and half a lime with chipped ice. Today, many people use Triple Sec instead of Cointreau. Both are made from fermented orange peels.

There already existed a popular drink called the Sidecar,

named after the famous motorcycles with a capsuled seat on the side. The Sidecar had a half moon of sugar on the rim of the glass. Since tequila goes with salt and lime, my Tío decided to wet the outer rim of the glass with a lime and sprinkle a full moon of salt. He is appalled when bartenders bury the whole rim of the glass in a dish of salt. It may look real pretty but I personally hate getting a mouthful of salt so I always have to wipe a clean entrance to the rim.

Another modern bad habit is the use of shaved ice to make a frozen Margarita. "It dilutes the liquor too much. You lose the bouquet."

Along with the Margarita, Tío Pancho also invented other drinks such as the now forgotten P29, P38, the Pancho Lopez and the Conga Cooler. The Margarita didn't have the immediate success that the Conga Cooler did. When Tommy's Place existed, there was a pink neon sign proclaiming it as the "Home of the Conga Cooler." Tío Pancho invented many drinks, many in honor of G.I.s' girl friends. As a young man Tío Pancho was a dead ringer for Bob Hope.

Francisco Morales was a first-rate bartender who could mix five hundred recognized drinks. "In seconds, a good bartender needed a fast memory . . . You also had to be fast and work long hours, from noon till four in the morning sometimes." The work took its toll on Tío Pancho's marriage and so he divorced my Tía Bibi. During the time that she lived, no one ever mentioned the Margarita drink in front of my Tía. Once I went shopping with her and separately I picked up a bottle of Margarita to purchase. As I was walking to join her at the register I remembered the family taboo, put it back on the shelf and picked a bottle of *Presidente.* She did read an earlier article I published on my Tío's invention and was very upset with me.

After his divorce, my Tío remarried a woman, who by coincidence was named "Margarita." When they were courting he told to her, "I'm a bartender, not a poet, so I named a drink after you."

After moving to El Paso from Juarez, Tío Pancho entered a Tequila Sauza mixed-drink contest for union bartenders. He sent them his Margarita recipe but was disqualified because the contest was for residents of Mexico only. He then applied for a copyright patent to his drink but neither the Mexican Government nor the U.S. Government recognized mixed drinks for granting patents.

Tequila Sauza representatives, who acknowledge his claim, annually visit the National Juarez Trade Fair and have invited him to have a drink. Remembering the disqualification, he always orders a Scotch.

My Tío has a small dilapidating cardboard box where he keeps articles about his claim including a newsprint receipt pad on the back of which are written many of his inventions: the Alejandrina was named after his first born daughter, the Delia after his first wife's cousin. There are newspaper and magazine clippings from around this country and Mexico testifying to his claim, including a piece in *Texas Monthly*. He showed me a *"Náchono Chografic"* (National Geographic) magazine where Señora Margarita Sauza is asked if the Margarita was named in her honor. She answers no, it was invented by a man in Northern Mexico. "She was sincere and honest," said my Tío. "She didn't mention the man's name or what part of *el norte* he was from."

I recently called to ask him what he thought about all these claims. He answered, "It used to bother me, but it doesn't any more." Nonetheless he doesn't quite understand some of these claims when they have no proof, in particular the woman who supposedly receives money from Cointreau for advertising their product. Tío Pancho also remembers an article in *Playboy* that gave credit to a woman from the state of Virginia, named Margarita, of course.

So who made the Margarita famous? "The people did," claims my Tío, "They're the ones that made it famous, *poco a poco,* little by little."

WHAT'S IN A SPANISH NAME?

The first time I ever ran across a Spanish word in Anglo-American literature was in grade school when we were assigned to read Mark Twain's "The Celebrated Jumping Frog of Calaveras County." It was a fun-filled, humorous story. Despite my home-honed fluency in *Español,* I did not recognize the Spanish word in the title and story.

I knew what a *calavera* was. It was a skull. For *el Día de los Muertos* in México, they were made into little skulls out of sugar and eaten like candy. In the Mexican game *Lotería, La Calavera* was illustrated with the crossed bones under the skull.

But within the context of an Anglo-American English class, in a school where Spanish was strictly forbidden and punishable by paddling, ridicule, and writing "I shall not speak Spanish in school" a hundred times, *calaveras* was pronounced anglo-phonetically *"kel-awe-ver-rahs."* The Spanish word Ca-la-ve-ras was hidden, disguised, nothing more than the name of a county. It was the mysterious name of an unknown person, place or thing. Innocently or naively, I took the word to be just another eccentric English word pronounced with a suave Anglo-American accent.

It took me a few years to discover that Calaveras County in California had been named for *Río Calaveras,* where a great number of skulls and skeletons had been discovered by early Spanish explorers.

Like Calaveras, hundreds of Spanish words remained in this country, changed, unchanged and disguised due to loss of meaning, evolution of misspellings, and mispronunciations. After 1848, when the U.S. took over the Southwest, Spanish had to survive on its own.

There's a town in Texas named Buda. With a Texas accent it is pronounced Bew-da. On the highway from Austin (pronounced Awe-stn or *Ostin* in Spanish) to San Marcos, pronounced Sanmar-cuss, there's a sign announcing Buda. That shouldn't have been odd but being from Texas it just didn't seem right. I could have understood Buddha or even Buttocks, Texas, but Buda?

It didn't take much ask'n before learning that the name was originally *Viuda,* which is Spanish for widow. Some monolingual Texan just didn't know any better and wrote it down just the way he heard it. That's how we got lariat from *la rieta,* hoosegow from *juzgado,* and buckaroo from *vaquero.*

What's Polamas? That's a street in San José, California. It's actually supposed to be Palomas, pigeons, but the person doing the lettering on street signs just didn't know better.

The Bank of America put out some cute little refrigerator magnets the size of a business card for its Spanish speaking clients where they could write important telephone "Numberos." Numberos? That's neither English, Spanish or Caló. The biggest bank in the U.S. of A. meant *números.* Even though it may have been an innocent bilingual typo, would you trust them with your *dinero?*

The one that has always troubled me is the English "tamale" pronounced tamalee. The Spanish singular for this food item is *tamal,* plural tamales. Don't go to the English language experts because Meriam-Webster's New Collegiate Dictionary also misspells tamale and its etymological rationale is that it comes from the Aztec Nahuatl *tamallí.*

Sarape is another such word. Webster says it's *serape,* but in the Spanish speaking world everyone pronounces it and spells it as sarape. Look it up in an English-Spanish dictionary or a Spanish-English dictionary and it's "sarape" in Spanish and "serape" in English. Why?

Throughout the last century and a half Spanish has had

free rein, running wild, with complete freedom to produce some mighty interesting words and sounds, not only from Gringos but from Mexicans themselves. Murrieta is now spelled Murieta, Monterrey is now spelled Monterey and Arrastradero is now spelled arastradero. Why anyone decided to take away the rolling "r" from so many of the Spanish words is beyond *moi.* Did someone find the extra "r" unnecessary, were they in short supply of r's, or was it just too difficult to roll their r's in Spanish?

In addition, words from 16th-century Spanish still roam throughout the Southwest, along with Caló, the Chicano dialect. These words have flourished and even emigrated back to Mexico where they have become part of the popular vernacular of the masses. The opposite also happens in Mexico and France and the rest of the world for that matter.

Though there may be many innocent reasons for this evolution of language, the isolation and syncretism, fusion of two cultures in language is fascinating.

I ran across a word in Mexico that is related to this argument but couldn't find in any dictionary, much less a synonym. It was *resemanticización* — resemanticization, also absent from any English dictionary.

Resemanticization was not defined but it was derived from the word "semantics"—the historical and psychological study and classification of changes in the meaning of words or objects. In politics and cross cultural situations, words, ideas and objects constantly assimilate, "transculturate," or adapt for the sake of survival.

Thus the anglicization or hispanization of words in this

country. The word "Chicano" was a resemanticized term that was once pejorative. Alurista, an early Chicano poet, resemanticized many words such as Aztlán, the ancient place of origin for the Aztecs was and is the Southwest. Amerindio came to describe not only an "American" Indian but all Indigenous peoples across the continent.

Chicano film, art and literature constantly redefines, resemanticizes, an experience that is part Anglo, part Español, part Mexicano. Resemanticization is also the exploitation of connotation and ambiguity in propaganda. Resemanticization deals not only with words but with ideas and symbols, that cross borders and languages to take different meanings.

We become chameleons, we are chameleon. As we move from one world to the other we exchange colors, ideas, symbols and words in order to fit, to relate and to survive. The result is a prismatic iridescence when the difference of colors play on each other, like a rainbow after a rainstorm in the desert. We are chameleons.

NUESTRA SEÑORA DE GUADALUPE: THE LEGEND AND THE IMAGE

She is everywhere. On T-shirts, tattooed on biceps and chests, etched into the back windows or lacquer enameled on the back trunks of low-riders, on murals, on tiles and medals. Even on cowboy boots. An El Paso boot maker designed such a pair that sell for $1,500, although the workers had to be convinced of the propriety.

After four hundred years as a private and highly revered religious figure, *Nuestra Santísima Señora de Guadalupe,* venerated Mother of Jesus

Christ, Mother of Mexico, Mother of the Americas, *La Morenita, La Guadalupana, Lupita,* Champion Mother of *La Raza*, has become a popular and recognizable figure in this country. Her image is devoutly and irreverently collected in various artistic styles and shapes. Within and outside her *Raza* community She has grown as a popular icon.

I have a hard time gauging what She represents as an icon or pop figure after growing up in a home where She was enshrined in a gold-colored frame. Her story was engraved into my conscious and subconscious. My mother and sister were named Guadalupe.

Our Lady of Guadalupe listens, comforts and protects, She is wisdom and innocence. She is a refuge for the forsaken. She is hope and aspiration. She is a symbol of belonging. She is God's closest intermediary. If you need anything, you approach God the Father through His closest adviser. Our Lady of Guadalupe has played a profoundly important role in the history and development of the Indio-Hispanic.

The legend of Nuestra Señora de Guadalupe is part of Raza history. Father Virgilio Elizondo, a Chicano and eminent theologian, describes this legend as part of our folklore, an important part of the history that lives in the collective spirit of its people. Religious folklore allows us to commune with what is essential to us, the divine. Through this communion we find meaning, pertinence and power.

Father Elizondo recognizes the impossibility of proving the legend of Our Lady of Guadalupe. Ten years after Hernán Cortes had entered and occupied present day

Mexico City, Tenochtítlan was in total chaos. That year, 1531, a dramatic event occurred that provided Mexico with a soul and a sense of order and unity it so desperately needed. La Virgen de Guadalupe appeared to Juan Diego.

The story is as popular and significant as any historical event in Mexico. Many Mexicanos, Chicanos and Latinos remember the legend from their mothers or grandmothers. In my parents' bedroom was the framed image of Our Lady of Guadalupe and on each corner of the image was a colorful oval illustration of the four apparitions.

During the early Saturday morning of December 12, 1531, Juan Diego, a fifty-seven year old Meshica Indian, traveled on foot to hear Mass in Tlatelolco. Seven years before the apparition, Juan Diego and his wife María Lucía had become Catholics. As he approached a hill called Tepeyac, he heard the beautiful music of birds. An unbelieving Juan Diego was perplexed, thinking he might be in a dream or that it had come from the terrestrial paradise that his ancestors, the elders, had promised. He looked East, to the crest of Tepeyac from where the sounds were coming when he heard his name, "Juanito, Juan Dieguito."

He climbed the hill and when he reached the summit he saw a woman standing. She asked him to come closer. Standing closer Juan Diego marveled at Her spiritual aura. As described by Juan Diego, Her clothing radiated like the sun, the rocks where She stood became jewels that dazzled and the ground lit up like a rainbow. The mesquite trees, cactus and green shrubs took on the appearance of emeralds, the foliage as fine turquoise, the branches and thorns shined like gold. He bowed his head. Her words, soft and gracious, alluring and reverent, asked where he was going.

Juan Diego responded, "Señora, I have to go to your house in Tlatelolco, Mexico, to pray as our priests, *delegados de Nuestro Señor,* teach us."

She then informed him of Her will, "Know and understand that I am forever the Holy Virgin Mary, Mother of the True God. . . . Without delay, I desire that a temple be built here in order to demonstrate all my love, compassion, help and protection to my children who reside on this land. In my temple, invoke my name and confidence. I will listen to their sorrows and remedy their miseries.

"Go to the palace of the Bishop of Mexico and promptly tell him all that you have seen and admired and what you have heard.

"I will be most grateful and you will be rewarded with great happiness. You have heard my command, my son; go forth with all your effort."

Juan Diego bowed, "My Señora, I will comply with your wishes. I say farewell, me your humble servant." Juan Diego climbed down and headed out on the road to México City.

Upon arriving, Juan Diego went directly to the Bishop's palace and immediately begged the servants to see Fray Juan de Zumárraga, a Franciscan priest. After a good long wait, he was invited into the Bishop's chambers.

Juan Diego bowed, kneeled in front of Bishop Zumárraga and excitedly gave him the message from the lady in heaven. He also described all he had admired and heard. The bishop remained unconvinced but seeing his excitement and sincerity, he asked Juan Diego to come back another day.

Juan Diego returned to the top of Tepeyac at once and upon seeing the Lady from Heaven he lay prostrate before Her, "Señora, I complied with your wishes. I entered the Bishop's office with much difficulty; I saw him and presented your message, just as you asked; but he seemed not to be convinced. . . . By the manner in which he responded he thinks I have invented this story. I beg of you, Señora, send an important person, known, respected and esteemed, to take your message so that he will believe it. You very well know that I am a nobody, a humble common man, a step ladder, a pile of dry leaves. You have ordered me to go where I don't belong. Forgive me for causing you grief and anger my Lady."

The Virgin responded, "Listen, my son, I have many servers and messengers to whom I could confide this message, but it is you who I wish to solicit for your help and mediation to fulfill my wish. I must order you to return again tomorrow to see the bishop. Greet him on my behalf and let him know my wish, that he has to begin work on the temple. And tell him again, that I, in person, the Perpetual Holy Virgin Mary, Mother of God, have sent you."

Juan Diego responded, "Señora, with good will, I will comply with your order. I will do as you wish. But maybe I will not be heard with pleasure, or if I am heard, perhaps he will not believe me. But I will return here tomorrow, when the sun sets, to give you his response."

The next day he went to the Bishop's palace. And once again, with great difficulty, he was finally able to obtain an audience with Bishop Zumárraga. This time, the Bishop interrogated him, where he lived, who he was . . . The Bishop listened attentively but was still not convinced. Juan Diego's word was not enough. He asked for proof that it was really the Lady from Heaven who had sent Juan Diego.

Without hesitation, Juan Diego responded, "Señor, what sign would you like? I will ask the Lady from Heaven who sent me here."

Bishop Zumárraga noted his confidence. He ordered his servants to follow him and to report back where he had gone and whom he had talked to.

Juan Diego, again, went directly to Tepeyac and the servants followed him. As they began to climb Juan Diego dropped out of sight. The servants searched for him to no end. So they returned to the bishop, tired and angry. They begged the Bishop not to believe Juan Diego arguing that his story was fabricated.

Juan Diego reported back to the Virgin.

"Bien *está, hijito mío.* Return tomorrow so that you can take the Bishop the sign he has asked for. He will no longer doubt or suspect you; and know that I will take care of you for the work and effort you have expanded for me. Go now and tomorrow I will await you."

The next day, Juan Diego's uncle was gravely ill. So Juan Diego spent the whole day trying to find a *médico* without success. Not finding a doctor, he decided to go to Tlatelolco the next day to find a priest who would come hear his

Uncle's confession and administer last rites. At dawn the next morning, Tuesday, December 12, 1531, Juan Diego set out for Tlatelolco unable to keep his appointment with the Lady from Heaven. To avoid seeing Her, Juan Diego decided to go around Tepeyac. But as he walked past the foot of Tepeyac, the Lady came down the hill, "What has happened, *hijo mío el más pequeño? ¿A donde vas?"*

Juan Diego was embarrassed, but he bowed and greeted Her, "Señora, I hope you are happy because I am going to cause you sorrow. Know that one of your children, my uncle, is very ill. I must go to your house in Mexico to call on one of the priests to confess my uncle and give him the last rites. But as soon as I finish, I will return here for your message. Señora, forgive me; please be patient, tomorrow I will come right away.

The Virgin responded, "Listen and understand, *hijo mío,* what frightens and afflicts you is nothing. Do not fear any illness or anxiety. Am I not here? Am I not your Mother? Are you not in my shadow? Am I not your health? Are you not on my lap? What else do you need? Do not worry about anything; your uncle will not die; know that he is already well."

These words lifted Juan Diego's spirits. She ordered him to climb to the top of the hill and to bring back the flowers he would find. He immediately obeyed and upon reaching the crest he was amazed by the variety of *rosas de Castilla* which were out of season. The roses were fragrant and covered with dew. He cut them and put them in his *tilma,* his coarse cloak made from threading the *maguey* plant. Juan

Diego then descended the hill and presented them to the Lady from Heaven. She held them in her hand and then placed them back in his tilma, saying, "*Hijo mío,* those flowers are the proof and sign you will take to the Bishop. Tell him these are a sign of my will. You are my ambassador, worthy of my confidence. I order you to open your tilma in front of the Bishop only. You will tell everything; how you got the flowers and all you saw and admired. This will induce the bishop to build the temple I have requested."

Juan Diego journeyed to the Bishop's house, happy and confident he would be believed without difficulty. But upon arriving, the Bishop's servants refused him entry, ignoring him. After a long while, when the servants saw that he was not going to leave, they informed the bishop. Soon the fragrance of the roses began to escape and the servants were able to detect what he had with him. Three times the servants tried to grab at the cloak but Juan Diego hung on tightly. The servants informed the Bishop who realized he might be carrying the Lady's sign, so he immediately agreed to see *el indio.*

Juan Diego greeted the Bishop with reverence and related all he had seen and admired. Then he gave him the Virgin's message, "Señor, I did as you ordered me, I told my Lady from Heaven, Holy Mary, precious Mother of God, that you asked for a sign so that you would believe me, that you should erect a temple where She has asked you to build it. I also told Her that I had given you my word that I would bring a sign and proof of Her will. She consented to your message and graciously agreed.

"I knew the top of the hill was not a place to find flowers because there is nothing but rocks, thistles, cactus and mesquite, but I did not doubt Her . . ."

Juan Diego opened his tilma. As the roses fell to the floor, the image of the Virgin Mother appeared on his coarse tilma.

Bishop Zumárraga and all who were present fell to their knees. The Bishop's eyes came close to tears as he asked forgiveness, not having followed Her will and command. He then stood up, loosened the cloak from Juan Diego and placed it in his private oratory and prayed. The Bishop ordered his assistants to begin plans for the temple immediately. Juan Diego stayed with the bishop until the next day, at which time he requested his leave to go see his gravely ill uncle whom the *Señora del Cielo* was to cure. They didn't allow him to return alone but accompanied him.

Arriving home, Juan Diego found his uncle happy and without pain. Juan Bernardino related how the Lady had also appeared to him at approximately the same time and explained that She had sent Juan Diego to see the Bishop. She also instructed Bernardino to go see the Bishop and to relate to him all he had seen and the miraculous manner in which he had been cured and that She should be named, as Her blessed image should be named, the perpetual *Virgen Santa María de Guadalupe."*

This request presented a problem because after the apparition there was much controversy and discussion about calling her Tonantzín, Nuestra Señora de Tepeyac, Tepeaquilla or Guadalupe. Such contradictions are common throughout the various studies, including one story of a Virgen de Guadalupe already existing in Guadalupe, Spain.

The Bishop's assistants returned to his palace with Juan Diego and his uncle who stayed until the temple of the Queen of Tepeyac was built. The Bishop then moved the holy image from the oratory in his palace to the main altar so the people could see and admire Her. The entire city was moved and marveled at such a divine miracle; no one on earth had painted that precious image.

Juan Diego lived for another seventeen years in a humble shed close to the church. He spent the rest of his life caring for the church grounds, fasting and in meditation. He died in 1548, at the age of seventy-four.

Interpretation of the Image

Virgilio Elizondo's, treatise on Nuestra Señora de Guadalupe, entitled "La Morenita—Evangelizadora de las Américas," is an important interpretation of the legend and images as it relates to the Mexicano, Mexican American and other indigenous peoples. From time to time in the following text, Elizondo and other Guadalupenologists are quoted.

Even before the apparition of Nuestra Señora, Tepeyac was one of the most venerated religious sites of the old world. At the top of the hill was a sanctuary consecrated to the Virgin Mother of the Gods, named Tonantzín. Tonán meant "mother earth." People came from afar to offer sacrifices to the Mother of the Gods.

Tonantzín represented the duality of human existence:

death and life. She represented life in death and death in life. Though these representations may seem to be contradictory, both form part of one. Tonantzín represented a future life in the certainty of this mortal world. Tonantzín best understood human suffering and with this wisdom was able to understand and console people in the midst of their sorrows and numerous life conflicts. In pre-Hispanic thought and culture, feminine deities were dual creators, of life and death, sensuality and purification, earth and water, destruction and protection. This is not at all different from what *La Guadalupana* represents.

The Virgin was named Nuestra Señora de Guadalupe rather than Nuestra Señora de Tepeyac because of the fear that people might continue the worship of the old Tonantzín. Also, a Virgen de Guadalupe de Extremadura, España, had accompanied the Conquistadors, many who were from Extremadura, Spain, including Hernan Cortes. They devoutly worshipped Her. It was also proposed to name her Nuestra Señora de Tepeaquilla.

Fray Bernardino de Sahagún who documented much of the ancient Mexican culture was aware of the Temple built for Nuestra Señora de Guadalupe and aware that the Indians still called her Tonantzín. "That has to be remedied," he wrote. Many Indians still remembered the Aztec Goddess Tonantzín and were familiar with her ancient image. To Sahagún, this was idolatry of a pagan past. Today only Tonantzin's head of stone remains; many Mexicanos still call her Our Lady of Guadalupe Tonantzín.

Another Goddess also venerated at Tepeyac was

Coatlicue (Koah-tlee-kooeh), *la mujer serpiente,* wearing a skirt made of serpents. To understand what the serpent meant to ancient Mexicanos, it is important to keep in mind that the serpent did not have the same Judeo-Christian biblical interpretation. For the indigenous, the snake did not represent deceit or evil, but the opposite. The scientific Mayas designed their complex system of geometry by studying the rattler's life cycle, geometric designs and its symbolism. Based partly on this system they built their temples and observatories and traced the movement of celestial bodies, thus designing a calendar that is .00001 more exact than the Julian Calendar.

The serpent regenerates every year and thus she was a symbol of death, on the path to resurrection. The snake did not seek to do harm but if stepped on it would defend itself—"don't tread on me or I will strike back." It represents human peace based on the respect for the rights of others. Mexican President Benito Juarez, a full-blooded Zapotec Indian was aware of this when he made his famous quote, "Peace is respect for your neighbors' rights." To the present day, the Mexican government's foreign policy reflects that belief. Coatlicue, the woman serpent, was considered the woman of wisdom, perfection and peace.

In ancient Mexico, the Indians built pyramids on top of pyramids. When the Spaniards occupied Tenochtítlan, they built their churches on top of the pyramids. Today one can still see some of the church stones on the outside walls with Aztec carvings.

Likewise, the temple for Nuestra Señora was built on the

ancient sanctuary for Tonantzín and Coatlicue. Tepeyac was also situated in the poorest region outside Mexico City where many destitute Indians lived. Like Juan Diego, they traveled on foot to Tenochtítlan for religious services.

The apparition of Nuestra Señora de Guadalupe came at a time when the Indian culture and spiritual way of life were crumbling before their very eyes. Juan Diego had been born with the name Cuauhtlatoactzin (Koo-wow-tla-toa-tzin) from *cuauhtli,* eagle, and *tlatoa,* to speak, he who speaks like an eagle. Tzin was an added diminutive of affection for Cuahtlatoac.

There is an interesting parallel between Juan Diego and St. John the Baptist, also known as the Eagle of Patmos. St. John the Baptist saw the Virgin surrounded by the sun, a moon and twelve stars around her head. Juan Diego could be called the Eagle of Tepeyac who saw the Virgin in like manner, dressed by the sun with the moon at her feet and dressed with a constellation of forty-six stars.

Virgilio Elizondo explains that Juan Diego saw "... not an *española* but an Indian." The legend tells us that her beauty left Juan Diego speechless. She had a young face but with very mature eyes and a smile filled with compassion. For the Mexicano, the face reflected the character of the person.

"The Virgin's tunic was a pale red. It was the color of Huitzilopochtli (Wee-tzi-lo-poch-tli) the sun God that preserved life and fed on the precious liquid of living blood. In 1487, in the Meshica year eight Acatl, Juan Diego was thirteen years old and likely present at the dedication of the great Teocali or *Templo Mayor de Tenochtítlan,* during the reign of Emperor Ahuizotl. He must have witnessed the bloody ceremony in which more than 80,000 captives were sacrificed.

Elizondo interprets the colors on the Virgin's image: "... red was also the color of the east from where the sun rises victorious after having died during the night. It is the color of its arrival and its departure, a continuity, the color of life through death, from a new beginning to a resurrection.

Elizondo continues, "The predominant color of the Virgin is her blue-green mantle, the color of Ometéotl, mother-father of the Gods, the origin of all the natural forces. This turquoise color was reserved for divinities and kings. In the psychology of the indigenous world, blue-green represented the center of a cross between two opposite forces. It symbolized fertility and life which come from opposite tensions."

The stars on her cloak had a very important significance. An Aztec prophecy had predicted that a comet would signal an end to their civilization. Ten years prior to the Spanish invasion of 1519, a forty-five year old Juan Diego must have been awestruck. The comet was visible even during the day. It was a good and bad premonition: the end of their civilization and the beginning of another. In the Aztec concept of time, each period had its own God. This was to be the era of la Señora.

In the indigenous culture, only VIPs such as royalty or representatives of the Gods were transported on the shoulders of another. Thus, being on top of a child angel meant that La Virgen had come on Her own from heaven and not with the Spanish ..."

The sun's rays shined around Nuestra Señora and although She hides the sun She does not extinguish it. The sun is Huitzilopochtli and Her red tunic represents the sacrificed blood to the Sun God.

The Virgin's eyes look at the people, unlike the eyes of other impersonal Gods who looked up or straight ahead. They express humility and compassion, a semblance of piety and understanding. She was beautifully human or humanly beautiful.

The black maternity ribbon around Her waist was a sign that She was expecting a child and offered it to the New World. Today Our Lady of Guadalupe has become a symbolic icon for the right to life, anti-abortion movement in this country. Difficult to distinguish in the area of Her navel is an indigenous cross representing the four directions, This symbolized that She carried the new nucleus of the universe within, the temple of the new presence of God . . .

Above and around Her collar is a Christian cross announcing that though She was an Indian, She was bringing Christ. This cross was a direct relation between the new God, loving and merciful and the *Señora Celestial.* She manifested truths more profound than those the missionaries had ever been able to express.

Interpretation of the Drama

Elizondo interprets the words, scenes and sounds of the drama. The music that Juan Diego first heard and the miraculous flowers as signs of Her apparition were symbolic for the Aztecs. *Flores y canto,* flowers and songs, were the most supreme and perfect communication. For the indigenous world, flowers and music signaled the presence of a creative power. The drama began with music and ended with flowers.

"Juanito, Juan Dieguito"—The Virgin called a vanquished Indian with loving tenderness. He was among the most oppressed by the Aztecs and the Spanish. He did not consider himself well born, educated, dignified or capable of anything important.

The apparition took place in one of the most famous and venerated hills in Mesoamerica. The beautiful Señora stood in the place of Tonantzín.

Elizondo: "If the invasion of Mexico was a tremendous victory for the Spanish, for the Mexicanos it was a catastrophic disaster. . . . But now, in the same place where the feminine aspect of the one and only almighty creative spirit had been venerated, something new was born. Their ancient pantheon of divinities had ended, their cult had been suppressed and their temples had been destroyed. This was the resurrection of a new life. From the ashes of the past a new road would continue.

"Mother of the true God, through whom one lives." The last part of this phrase, "through whom one lives," is very much a part of the Catholic faith but for the indigenous it was even more of a way of life. God not only created life but also maintained it."

The Virgin's wish for a temple was not so much a physical stone and mortar building but a more living temple of people that the Franciscans had been unable to accomplish. It was to be the living temple, the collective conscience of *la nueva raza.*

In essence, Nuestra Señora de Guadalupe did not subdue or pacify but was a dynamic and living force, a call for action and a powerful symbol of unity. She effected the personal love and esteem of *la raza,* bringing them *liberación y paz.*

The trauma had begun with "conquest" and the violation of their women. Elizondo explains, "Only through heavenly intervention could the conquest and oppression of Mexico be revoked. A people, truly proud of their existence begins not from a violated person but through a celestial mother, pure and immaculate. This compassionate mother would remedy the worst miseries, sorrows and laments . . .

"She responds to the most profound instincts of the Mexican: an obsession for legitimacy and the sensitivity of being an orphaned people. Thus, through the Virgin of Tepeyac, the Mexicanos found the realization of their most intimate aspirations . . . the spiritual emancipation of a new Mexican nation, one which years later would give the strength and courage to declare its independence from the mother country . . ."

On September 15, 1810, Father Miguel Hidalgo y Costilla, tore an image of Our Lady of Guadalupe from a church painting, bound it to a lance and proclaimed Mexico's Cry for Independence, today known as *El Grito,* the cry for independence, with the words, *"¡Viva Nuestra Señora de Guadalupe! ¡Death to the gachupines!"*

At this point, Mexico and likewise Our Lady of Guadalupe proclaimed their total independence from

Spain. She became strictly and totally Mexicana. For this "treason" Father Miguel Hidalgo was excommunicated by the Catholic Church and eventually executed by the Spanish Government in Chihuahua, Chihuahua, today just four hours south of the U.S. border.

In 1828 the Mexican Congress declared each twelfth of December a national holiday. In 1910, Pope Pius declared the Virgin of Guadalupe, "Patroness of Latin America."

La Virgen en Los Estados Unidos

The Virgin of Guadalupe has been venerated throughout the Southwest up to and since 1848 when the United States plundered close to half of Mexico's territory and then made it official through the Treaty of "Guadalupe" Hidalgo. After 1848, the Virgin in the U.S. was nothing more than a private and familial Virgin. Considering Her popularity, there are a few churches named after her. In other Anglo-American or Irish-American churches around the Southwest She is given a corner or wall space for Her image.

But it was not until the United Farm Worker struggle headed by Cesar Chavez that the Virgin became a public figure in this country. Throughout the UFW marches, strikes and pilgrimages, three icons stand out: the UFW black eagle, portraits of Emiliano Zapata, revolutionary hero of Mexico's campesinos and la Virgen de Guada-lupe. La Guadalupana becomes the new Mother of Chicanos as a symbol of identity, spiritual power, liberation and unity. She began to appear in murals, silk screens, sculptures, poems and songs of El Movimiento Chicano.

In the seventies, Yolanda Lopez, Chicana artist from San Diego, completed a series of paintings on la Virgen de Guadalupe. Each painting transforms the Virgin into another concept, totally foreign and sacrilegious to the most faithful of Mexico. In one painting, the Virgin is a matronly Mexican woman in conservative high heels. In another She is an Indian woman breastfeeding a child. In another, Yolanda Lopez's grandmother sits at a sewing machine making the Virgin's star studded cloak. In still another, La Virgen becomes the artist herself, jogging, cloak flying behind her, a snake in her hand, and stepping on the little angel.

Yolanda Lopez brought theVirgin down from the altar and humanized her. The Virgin retains Her identity and attributes, but also demonstrates Her humanity by engaging in common everyday circumstances. She reclaims equality and justice for herself, for women, for men, and for Chicanos. The distinction between the Mexican and the Chicano versions of La Virgen are now distinct.

These "resemanticized, reconceptualized," images of the Virgin of Guadalupe in the Chicano experience had more visibility, impact and notoriety in Mexico than they did in this country. Yolanda had changed the significance and spiritual commonplace of the sacred icons. Chicanos, so far in distance from the Mother Country felt the freedom to explore the image that Mexicanos had taken for granted for so long and dared not desecrate.

La Virgen de Guadalupe has been taken from the home to the public domain, to the Mexico within the U.S.

Approximately ten years after Yolanda's Guadalupe series, another Guadalupe work of art was produced and exhibited in Mexico. Inspired or influenced by Lopez, one Mexican artist painted the Virgin with the face of Marilyn Monroe. On another painting of the Last Supper, Christ's face was replaced with the face of the late Mexican actor Pedro Infante. A great number of Mexico City people were outraged. The faithful knelt and prayed, keeping vigil outside the museum gallery until the "offending" art work was removed.

The different interpretations between the Yolanda Lopez Guadalupe series and the Marilyn Monroe Guadalupe are fascinating. Was the Mexican Marilyn "Monroe-ization" of Our Lady of Guadalupe a follow-up to the Chicano humanization? Yolanda Lopez retained the Mexican-style of the Virgin while the Mexican artist turns her into a glamorous Hollywood icon. It speaks volumes about the saturated influence of Hollywood and U.S. culture in Mexico. The new religion of glamour and consumerism from *El Norte*. While Chicanos struggle, and in many cases succeed, to preserve their identity in the U.S., Mexicanos realize their own futility. Nuestra Señora de Marilyn Monroe is more than a mocking satire of the encroaching Anglo-American culture on Mexico's evolution from an ancient indigenous culture. It speaks to the innocence and crucifixion of women.

It's almost a return to Tonantzín. The gallery becomes another Tepeyac where one Virgin dies and another is born. Her primary identification is with the indigenous, with the Mexicanos, with the Chicanos. Initially, She was able to unite the Indian with the Criollo and the Spaniard. In this country, She unites Chicanos with Mexicanos besides giving Chicanos a sense of unity, power and belonging. Elizondo explains how the Virgin encourages self dignity, confidence and direction. She facilitates reconciliation and cooperation without losing identity. She inspires confidence, faith and love.

On a personal note, I have literally lived under her image all through my childhood. The Anglo-American nuns reinforced her value to their Mexican-American students. She stood out on processional banners.

Nuestra Señora de Guadalupe was always present in times of trouble. At the age of eight, on a family trip to Chihuahua we stopped on the highway where a truck had turned over. The driver survived without a scratch. I remember looking into the cab resting on its roof. A good sized statue of the Virgin, also upside down, had been tied just above the rear view mirror.

Even earlier when my parents and their four children slept in one bedroom in the basement of a synagogue I remember once opening my eyes from a peaceful sleep to see the Virgin by the door. She wasn't radiant like Juan Diego described, but peaceful, quiet and shadow-like. I was slightly scared and so I closed my eyes and went to sleep again. The next day I forgot all about it until my sister Guadalupe mentioned to our aunt in Juarez how she had seen the same image. Our aunt laughed, wondering how *La Virgencita* could ever appear in *los Estados Unidos.* Regardless of whether it was a paranormal delusion or auto suggestive dream, it did have an effect.

In later life, I came to realize that Nuestra Señora de Guadalupe had been nothing more than a church ploy, a plot, a device to convert the Indians. How could I have believed in such a story? What about Tonantzín?, I asked. I wanted to put Tonantzín before the Virgin of Guadalupe. But it was impossible. She was too much a part of me so I began to heal the sense of betrayal by reading about Nuestra Señora de Guadalupe, about Tonantzín, and Coatlicue, about the conquest. Understanding Yolanda Lopez's images, I no longer believed in blind faith but I again believed in Her.

Today I carry Her image in my car, confident when She is in sight. She soothes me when I look at Her. Perhaps it is nothing more than the affirmation I recall from my childhood memories as I draw Her, paint Her, collect Her and contemplate Her.

Just as we need a real father on earth and God as a divine father; just as we need a tangible and physical mother on earth, just as we need the elderly wisdom and tenderness of a grandmother, we also need a divine mother—Nuestra Señora de Guadalupe.

QUETZALCOATL

In San José, California, the City Council approved a sculpture of Quetzalcoatl (pronounced ket-zal-ko-atl) by Mexican sculptor Robert Graham for Cesar Chavez Park. From the beginning, protests erupted from various segments of the community including some Chicanos who felt the money could have been spent on their community needs.

In November, 1994, the sculpture was unveiled amidst protests by right-wing religious zealots who denounced Quetzalcoatl as an ancient blood-thirsty God. Following the unveiling, the media picked up the protests and they became even more vile and vicious. Columnists and cartoonists had a field day calling it a mound of dog poo, coiled feces. A *San José Mercury* editorial wallowed in displeasure and called it a lump, "squat sculpture" lamenting that it was not a soaring, graceful bronze sculpture shooting up to heaven. The sculpture could not be appreciated from the sidewalk across the street.

Had these journalists been more familiar with Pre-Colombian art, had they visited *el Museo Arqueológico de México,* often called the most beautiful archeological museum in the world and home to thousands of pre-Colombian artifacts and sculptures they would have found many "squat sculptures" and many "lumps."

Robert Graham's sculpture of Quetzalcoatl captured the massive and unmovable spirit of Mesoamerica. It is close to the earth, like its people, it is the color of the earth, not of white doves or soaring chrome spirals. Quetzalcoatl is the connection between earth and sky, the plumed serpent. Its representation was recognized even in our own bodies: The spinal column reaches from our tail-end to our cerebrum, a reminder of our evolution as reptiles.

The sculpture brought one of this continent's greatest leaders to this country. Five hundred and two years after the Spaniards thought they had destroyed Quetzalcoatl, he joined his descendants in San José. Forgotten and dismissed were the hundreds of indigenous people that traveled from Mexico and throughout the Southwest to San

José to celebrate and honor Quetzalcoatl. There aren't that many indigenous sculptures in city parks but they are proud of this one, regardless of those who wanted soaring sculptures, something that would reflect Euro-American aesthetics.

The word, Quetzalcoatl, is a metaphor of sight and sound. The *Quetzal* is the name of a rare bird with green feathers inhabiting the highlands of Chiapas and Guatemala. *Co* means snake and *atl* means water.

Quetzalcoatl was the name of one of the greatest lords of all time. He was not a god but a human being, a lord, like Christ. He personified the forces of heaven, earth and water, a holy trinity not unlike the Christian Father, Son and Holy Ghost. Consider the image of Christ being baptized in the water and the Holy Ghost in the form of a dove above Him. The parallels to Christianity are many. Quetzalcoatl was associated with Tlaloc, the Rain God. Christ was baptized in water by John the Baptist.

The concept of bird, snake and water is also illustrated in Mexico's national symbol. An eagle devouring a snake, atop a cactus in the middle of a lake symbolizes the founding of Tenochtítlan by the Aztecs after migrating south from Aztlán. Birds and snakes have never co-existed peacefully and one of the very few birds capable of killing a snake is the giant eagle. These two animals represented the strong forces of heaven, the earth and the water.

Quetzalcoatl is credited with founding and creating one of the greatest civilizations in the world. A seminal figure in the history of Teotihuacán, Tula, Yucatán, Oaxaca and most other Mesomerican nations, Quetzalcoatl was the principal Lord of the Toltecas, Aztecas, Mayas, Quiches, Olmecas and other Mesoamerican Indians.

However, Quetzalcoatl was also a victim of the Spanish invasion of Mexico that forced implementation of the Roman Catholic dogma, Since then Quetzalcoatl has forever been unfairly maligned as an evil god who instituted human sacrifices. The truth—Quetzalcoatl was as gentle and life giving as Jesus or Buddha. He has been called "the moral hero and liberator of ancient Mesoamerica." Human sacrifices were never offered to Quetzalcoatl. They were offered to a God called Huitzilopochtli. According to Carlos Fuentes, that liberty was the light of knowledge and education, a light so powerful that it became the base of legitimacy for all.

Quetzalcoatl is credited with the creation of a calendar, a measure of time more precise than the Julian Calendar, the cultivation of corn, agriculture, the ethics and philosophy of Mesoamerican culture.

Quetzalcoatl was at one time a real historical person but as with most legends his attributes become many, varied and obscure to the point that time turned him into a God or a myth. Through Mesoamerican history, there are many other Quetzalcoatls, priests who were given his name or who took it.

The complexity of Quetzalcoatl and the number of other Quetzalacoatl priests and myths could never fit into this short essay. Nonetheless, this is a brief attempt to begin to appreciate part of that fascinating and brilliant ancient

Mesoamerican lord who gave so much to the world.

A religion and cult developed around Quetzalcoatl at the same time as the decline and disappearance of various religious centers and cities such as Teotihuacan around 750 and 900 A.D. Quetzacloatl was represented by the bird that symbolized the heavens; The serpent that symbolized celestial water, cloud or rain; A dissected shell containing the wind; As a divine spirit, as regeneration and birth, the totality of the universe, the four cardinal directions with the center.

It was at this time that Quetzalcoatl passed from not only the historical person but also as the god of cyclical time and of rain as Tlaloc. Various priests took the name of Quetzalcoatl and some became semi-lords.

One of those was Quetzalcoatl, the god of wind, Ehécatl and creator of the first man and woman of the fifth sun. According to one myth, Quetzalcoatl became intoxicated with his rival Texcatlipoca and lost his chastity. For this, Quetzalcoatl was cast from the Garden of Lords. Quetzalcoatl then journeyed to the sea and set himself afire.

Quetzalcoatl has also been called the Morning Star, or "One Reed." After his flaming death he descended to Mictlán, the place of death, battled successfully against satanic forces and returned with the bones of a man and a woman. He then stabbed himself with these bones and like Christ's death on the cross redeemed humanity from damnation.

As the planet Venus, Quetzalcoatl traveled daily to the other world in the West and then appeared every morning as the Morning Star in the East. It was Venus that inspired their calendar. Through observation and precise mathematical calculations it was noted that each cycle lasted 584 days.

Numerous representations of Quetzalcoatl on various pyramids and pre-Columbian artifacts from Teotihuacán in the high plateaus to Chichén Itzá in the Southern lowlands of Yucatán give testimony to his past existence. According to Tolteca legend, history and western calculations, Ce *Acatl Topiltzin,* better known as Quetzalcoatl was born in 947 B.C. This priest-king of Tula, the holy city of the Toltecas founded a religion which was to do away with human offerings. He replaced them with offerings of snails, birds, and butterflies. Quetzalcoatl was a great lawgiver, civilizer, creative in the arts and crafts, inventor of the calendar, or *Book of Fate*. He was a priest and a king. According to the writings in the *Codex Chimalpopoca,* devils constantly hounded him to kill and commit human sacrifices. He refused because he loved his Tolteca vassals. Eventually, Quetzalcoatl was banished from Tula by the "bloodthirsty worshippers of Texcatlipoca." His regime was followed by a reign of terror, hunger, war and pestilence in Mexico.

The complexity of Quetzalcoatl continues. He is seen as a ladder from heaven to earth with man at the center ("on the third day he arose from the dead and ascended into heaven"). Quetzalcoatl is said to have ascended to the planets to become part of the sun, the source of all life. As the sun, Quetzalcoatl became a male, impregnating Mother

Earth, to bring forth a son. In the Vienna Codex, there is a naked Quetzalcoatl suspended in heaven and receiving gifts from the Dual Lord and Lady above all. Quetzalcoatl as a ladder has also been compared to Hindu philosophy in its seven powers of nature.

When Luis Valdez founded El Teatro Campesino he authored a manifesto entitled Pensamiento Serpentino, a Chicano approach to the Theater of Reality. This Mayan philosophy was a serpentine concept of embracing time, constant evolution, growth and a future where a deep sense of continuity prevails. The serpent annually crawls out of its own dead skin. All living things evolve and change. Quetzalcoatl, the feathered serpent, unified the symbolic spirituality of the feathers with the earth serpent. All life is dynamic and in a state of constant motion, constant change, constant evolution. The mountain ranges, the valleys, the rivers and the coastlines were serpentine, all changing forever but always keeping their integrity. Quetzalcoatl became a symbolic savior, not a nostalgic or romantic figure but real.

In defense of Quetzalcoatl, George L Vásquez, a scholar of Latin American history and culture, stated, "Quetzalcoatl the legendary lord was a positive figure who embodied the sky and the rain which fell from it, as well as regeneration and the founding of the human race itself. The historical Quetzalcoatl was a leader who stressed social ethics and established a humanistic tradition which has lasted until today. He taught people how to sing, how to be good of heart . . ."

THE WORKING CLASS INTELLECTUAL

Eduardo Galeano, one of Latin America's many brilliant writers, doesn't appreciate being called a "political writer" though he acknowledges he is one. For Galeano, that term has damaging implications that limit and invalidate his literature, a literature that is boundless.

At the same time, Galeano doesn't care to be described as an "intellectual" because it is in direct opposition to manual labor. "That," he says,

". . .is a mutilation of the human being, an objective of the ruling class who have us convinced that there are people who are 'head' and others who are 'hands' . . . And I believe that we can be everything at once. I am political and many more things. I cannot cease being political because I am in solidarity with my own and because I hurt as if their needs were mine."

Eduardo Galeano strives for *"razón y corazon"* in his literature. He will explain how the cost of living is spiraling up in Latin America while the value of life is spiraling down.

In this world, and especially in this country, people and things are compartmentalized, classified and specialized. What are generally beautiful complex puzzles are taken apart piece by piece. Poet Bernice Zamora, illustrates it even further as a woman poet, "So not to be mottled": You insult me / When you say I'm / Schizophrenic. / My divisions are / Infinite.

Distinctions between intellectuals and activists do more damage than help to our communities. How many times have we heard parents praise the academic accomplishments of their children and then resign themselves to the humility of having a limited education and limited intellectualism? The children repeat these lessons taught so well by parental example. Some students become successful scholars and further distance themselves from their parents. So at some family Christmas dinner, the parents become nothing more than spectators, witnesses to a conversation they are not invited to join in.

Often enough though, children do not become successful scholars. One of the reasons for the high number of Chicano and Latino dropouts is parental non-involvement in schools. Latino parents do not have the sense of intellectual competence to question a foreign school system. They have complete trust in a school system that will inevitably fail at least five out of every ten of their precious children.

Too many working class parents, in the words of an anonymous socialist paper, "go through life believing that the world of ideas, of theory and science, is beyond their ability to understand. They believe theory and science have very little to do with their everyday lives or activities. They accept the idea that the world of ideas, the realm of thought, is for intellectuals and professionals . . . but it doesn't take a professional historian to understand the important changes of the past and the new changes coming about."

Some elitist academics have forever prided themselves on being the "ordained," paid to think full time for the working people. The sharp division between physical and mental labor reflects the present split between universities and their communities.

A national conference on Chicano art was planned by a border city. The organizers invited all the Chicano art critics with advanced degrees and who had written on Chicano art. Not one community artist from that town or any other town was invited. Yet they were going to discuss an art conceived by working class intellectuals from the community.

Of course, any time anyone mentions the "working class" there is alarm and fear, for it smacks of socialism.

But that's who starts all revolutions, struggles, strikes and organizations, intellectuals who are activists. How can you be passionate about an ideal with only your head, or only your hands? It just doesn't add up.

PRIMERO MAYO

Every first of May overflows with the certainty of life, a celebration of the sun season when flowers and blue skies sing a true *flor y canto, floricanto,* flower and song. The first of May rejoices in the rebirth of nature and the scent of flowers can take me back to grade school.

On the first of May a flower laden altar was built to the Virgin Mary in our catholic school classroom. May was the "Month of Mary," Mother of Jesus. The daily rosary was recited for the conversion of Communist Russia. It was during the fifties, they had the H bomb and worse, they didn't believe in God.

An annual May queen was chosen from class, usually the shyest girl who exemplified the holy virtues of the Virgin Mary, a straight A student with an A+ in Conduct. Her reward was to place a crown of flowers on the Virgin. At St. Patrick's, only two girls were deemed worthy of that honor and so they alternated each year. The other girls were alright, but it was the nuns who had the sole power to pick the queen. In some schools, the biggest parish contributor's daughter was picked. A church procession ended and all the girls, including the "less virtuous," became flower maidens strewing flower petals and offering bouquets to the Holy Virgin Mary.

A few years later in the military, May Day was transformed from a "Holy Day" to a "Holy Hell Day." Overseas, all military personnel were warned, advised or forbidden from stepping outside their bases on the first of May. It was Communist Day! Red Day! The day when communists roamed the streets of the world in search of Americans to beat up. Either that or if you possessed an American car, it would get stoned, smashed and burnt. I never heard of that happening but we had been duly forewarned, "Stay away from the natives!"

"Mayday! Mayday!"—the international words of distress on radio. Except for the Catholic Church, May Day was a bad day for this country.

But there was another memory back home on the border that I never much paid attention to. On the other side of el *Río Bravo, el primero de Mayo* was *el Día del Trabajador,* Workers' Day. *Trabajadores en México* not only enjoyed a holiday but they were feted, honored and celebrated.

Eventually I woke up to the fact that International Workers' Day is celebrated throughout the world each May the first. It is a public holiday in more than seventy nations around the world with one of the few exceptions being its place of birth, the United States. International Workers' Day is not only *not* celebrated in this country, but it is not even known or acknowledged. The rest of the world calls it many things: International Day of Solidarity of the Working People, Saint Joseph the Worker Day or the Eight Hours Day. Try to find out about May Day or the history of labor in this country at your local bookstore or library and see how far you get.

The history of May Day is long, complex and tragic. But it is also a triumphant victory of the workers' human spirit throughout the world.

There has always been a labor day celebration in this country but the days have varied. By the 1820s and 1830s, the Fourth of July had become the working class day of celebration. By the early 1880s, at different times, three labor days evolved: May Day, September 5 and the first Monday in September.

The first May Day was proclaimed at an 1884 convention of the Federation of Organized Trades and Labor Unions of the United States and Canada. They adopted a resolution asserting that eight hours would constitute "a legal day's labor from and after May 1, 1886."

That decision and the resulting campaigns produced many widespread strikes throughout the United States, Canada and Europe. On the target date of May 1, 1886, Chicago had one of the biggest rallies with approximately 90,000 demonstrators on the streets: 30,000 to 40,000 on strike and another 45,000 already having benefited from decreases in working hours. The strike paralyzed Chicago.

The infamous Chicago Haymarket Square demonstration of May 4, 1886 followed. On that afternoon, 180 policemen arrived in formation to halt the rally. In the process of attacking the crowd a bomb was thrown into the police formation. More than 60 policemen were wounded and one was killed. The crowd dispersed through the streets and the police shot indiscriminately, killing eleven people and injuring hundreds.

Despite a total lack of evidence, seven union organizers, today known as the Chicago martyrs, were "railroaded to the gallows." Four of the seven were executed by hanging: Albert B. Parsons, August Spies, Michael Schwab and Adolph Fischer.

Much was made of the fact that most of these men were foreign born. But it caught the jury by surprise when it learned that Albert Parsons' ancestors were passengers on the Mayflower, graduates of Harvard and Yale, a pastor of an early Congregational church, and important military figures in the Revolutionary War.

Albert Parsons served in the Confederate Army, settled in Waco, Texas and became a Radical Republican during Reconstruction, championing African American rights and mobilizing black voters. His courage earned him the respect of many, including the woman he married, Lucy Enedile Gonzalez as she sometimes called herself. Her ancestry and activism was in question even while she was alive, from 1853 to 1942.

Lucy Gonzalez Parsons has commonly been known as a Mexican American hero to Chicanos. However, one biographer, Carolyn Ashbaugh, states that Lucy Parsons was emphatically African American. A quick look at photographs of Lucy does confirm that she was African American. But there is also something, hauntingly Mexican and indigenous about her. Biographer Carolyn Ashbaugh herself describes Lucy Parsons, " . . .Her skin was golden brown, that of a mulatto or quadroon. One might believe that her piercing black eyes shot sparks when she was angry. She had soft sensuous lips, a broad nose, curly black hair, and the high cheekbones of her Indian ancestors." A Mexican is an Indian. Yet in her chapter notes, Ashbaugh writes, "On Lucy's death certificate her parents are listed as Pedro Diaz and María Gonzales. According to Ashbaugh, Lucy identified herself as Native American and Mexican in an effort to cover up her black heritage.

It is very possible that she could have been American Indian but there is no evidence or association to any particular tribe. The fact that she met Albert Parsons at a ranch close to Waco, Texas would definitely leave open the possibility of Mexican ancestry. Ranches in Texas employed a great number of Mexicanos. The cowboy profession itself evolved from *vaqueros* Mexicanos.

Lucy, Ashbaugh states, took the surname of Gonzalez for protection because Texas law banned "miscegenation," interracial marriage. Mexicanos didn't fare any better than African Americans in Texas.

Less we forget, it was the Spanish who introduced slavery on this continent and the word "negro."

The controversy over Lucy Parsons' ancestry is absurd. According to Philip S. Foner, author of *May Day*, International Publishers, she was a former slave of both African American and Mexican Indian descent. Rather than a controversy, Lucy Gonzales Parsons should be a matter of pride for Mexican Americans and African Americans to share a woman hero representing the working class. It is through the labor movement that one finds interracial harmony and solidarity.

But Lucy Parsons also suffered another kind of discrimination, that of being a woman. Because she was Albert Parsons' widow, Lucy has never been given due credit and recognition. On the contrary she has been vilified, even by labor historians. Yet if one considers her activism publishing newspapers, writing pamphlets and books, traveling to lectures and demonstrations right up to her 1942 death, at the age of ninety-two, some good must be said of her. At the founding convention of the Industrial Workers of the World, Lucy Parsons stated, ". . . men have been slaves throughout all the ages, but the woman's condition has been worse, for she has been the slave of a slave . . . We are the slaves of the slaves. We are exploited more ruthlessly than men . . ."

Lucy Eneldine Gonzales Parsons is an amazing figure in U.S. History who we know very little about. Consider Mother Jones, a contemporary Anglo- American colleague of Lucy's. Mother Jones even has a progressive magazine named after her.

Over a hundred years after the execution of Parsons, Spies, Fischer and Schwab, the forty-hour week is a taken-for-granted matter of fact around the world as we strive to shorten the week some more.

The stories of Fischer, Spies and Schwab are as important and fascinating as Albert and Lucy Parsons'. The inscription on those four sepulchers reads in part: "Here we guard the remains of the best of us. Here . . . sleep four generous men that dreamed of conquering humanity's welfare by virtue of their one act . . . Freedom is not won on your knees but afoot . . ."—words that echo a great Mexican hero, "It is better to die on your feet than to live on your knees," said Emiliano Zapata.

In this country, May 1 has never enjoyed the kind of celebratory tradition and ceremony that is has abroad. The reasons are many and worth recounting. They didn't all have to do with communism.

When the Puritans arrived on the Mayflower they objected to all secular celebrations. The Plymouth colony residents in New England were naturally scandalized when, on May 1, 1627, an Anglican named Thomas Morton erected an eighty- foot pine Maypole, decorated with flowers, ribbons and antlers. It was even rumored that Morton and his people had danced with Indian women. John Endecott, the

Puritan leader put a stop to the celebration and had the pole chopped down.

One of the main reasons International Workers' Day on May 1 never took hold in this country was fear of socialism. In 1882 the American Knights of Labor instituted Labor Day on the first Monday in September. After the 1884 convention proclamation and the resulting Haymarket Riots on May 4 1886, the rest of the world decided to honor May 1.

In Paris, 1889, an international labor convention resolved that a great international demonstration would be held at a fixed date, in every country and in every town. Workers would call upon the state for legal reduction of the working day to eight hours.

So on May 1, 1890, hundreds of large militant demonstrations were held throughout European capitals and industrial cities as well as in the United States.

Fearing continued socialism and labor unrest, the US Congress, in 1894, declared the first Monday in September as the official Labor Day, a designation that remains in force today.

Throughout the struggle for the eight-hour working day and improved worker benefits, there were bombs and bloody battles with police. Thus, May 1 became a rallying day for progressives, socialists and communists.

In 1896 the celebration spread throughout Russia when an imprisoned Lenin wrote a May Day leaflet that was distributed to the workers of 40 factories in St. Petersburg, a town which came to be called Leningrad. By May 1, 1914, one million Russian workers were participating in the May Day strikes.

After the successful revolution of 1917 the Russian communists chose May Day as the greatest of their holidays; and red, the color of May Day, as their flag. The communists used it as an occasion to laud their doctrines and rededicate themselves to the cause of the international proletariat, calling for the workers of the world to unite.

Thus the United States moved even further away from May Day. In 1947 the U.S. Veterans of Foreign Wars designated May Day as Loyalty Day on which to reaffirm loyalty to the United States. A joint resolution of the U.S. Congress officially designated May 1 of each year as Loyalty Day. All were urged to fly the red, white and blue.

If that wasn't enough, in 1958, President Dwight D. Eisenhower instituted Law Day on May 1 at the urging of the American Bar Association. Law Day is not Lawyers' Day but a direct attempt to emphasize the laws of the United States of America and to contrast them with those of "governmental tyranny under Communism."

Today the Communist Party and the Soviet Union are history. We could get back to honoring the Chicago Martyrs of 1886, honoring the eight-hour day, honoring the workers who built this country and bettered the lives of our parents and grandparents. And there are still plenty of workers who suffer at the hands of abusive and exploitative employers: from farmworkers and women in sweat shop industries, to young people in fast food restaurants.

As the 21st century begins to shadow the 20th, Chicano and Latino educational levels are the lowest. Consequently they have the lowest paying jobs. In the Sunbelt, Chicanos,

Mexicanos and Centroamericanos pick the crops, fry and broil the hamburgers, clean the offices, wash the dishes and serve the rest of the population. If history repeats itself, which it usually does, the techno-peasants of the 21st century will explode with labor unrest. It has already begun, through rural farmworkers and the urban janitors.

On May the first, Día del Trabajador, the rest of the world honors the worker, the people, the individual humans who toil, sweat and died, such as Parsons, Spies, Schwab and Fischer, for their families, their children and for their country. There is nothing communist about this. In New York City's Union Square, May Day rallies have been held since 1924. It should be reclaimed.

You may ask, what is wrong with our national Labor Day, the first Monday of every September? It has become meaningless and nothing more than a holiday and a marker. It marks the end of summer, the beginning of school, the beginning of Fall, it marks the beginning of Baseball's World Series, it's Labor Day sales at the department, drug and food stores. It is a big capitalist celebration. Labor Day celebrates the work, the labor, the product, not the worker, not the people who toiled to make this country great.

The first of May has been replaced by *El Cinco de Mayo*, that spring marker, a day when we celebrate a la Mexicana, without realizing we are celebrating *la primavera,* Spring, the season of colorful flowers and songs. As honorable and historically momentous as el Cinco de Mayo is, it still doesn't compare with the history and significance of the

First of May. It could honor our labor heroes: Parsons, Spier, Schwab, and Fischer, Lucy Gonzales Parsons, Cesar Chavez.

MÉXICO, LOVED AND SURREAL

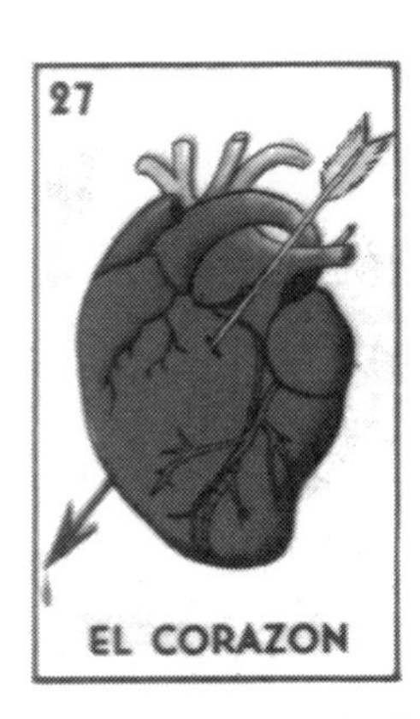

We lived on the border close enough to the Rio Bravo that as kids we hiked across a few rocky desert hills to wade in its cool running waters and fish for tiny minnows. Once a year, during the sweltering summer afternoons, the local paper annually carried a photo of someone frying eggs on a burning pavement as the *chicharras* sang the sizzle.

To escape that heat someone would drive us up the Río Grande into New Mexico and we would float down on black rubber tires. As the Río entered Texas from New Mexico it would also begin to flow between Mexico. From this side we would gaze at Mexico's vast powerful desert and raw mountains that daily reflect the New Mexico sunsets.

My father had known that desolate desert land across the river as a child. Everytime he drove us by the highway along the river he would point it out with an extended arm. "All that land," he would remind us in Spanish, "from that hill there with the adobe ruins all the way to those hills over there, all that land belonged to my father." My grandfather was supposedly a full-blooded indian who passed away in the great epidemic of 1918. "Who knows what tribe he belonged to, but he spoke his Indian language." In those days of the forties and fifties, the hills were empty desolate desert country. Today the area is populated and has progressed from poor ramshackle *colonias* without electricity or water to lower-middle-class homes.

He also knew the land on this side of the border just as well, for he was born in 1905 when Mexicanos migrated back and forth across the border, just as they had done for centuries, following the crops, the seasons and the reasons. Like my parents, I too had to migrate out of El Paso to find the cash crops, the seasons and the reasons after my graduation. My departure, my physical proximity to that border, has lessened since I left but I have returned to Mexico many times, more intimately and intensely. And in California more than ever, I discover the secret this country denies. Mexico never left.

I had not seen my father since 1986 and then in 1991, by the strangest coincidence, I ran into him on a trip to Mexico City, the biggest and largest city in the world, with over 20 million souls. I came upon him by a one to 20 million chance.

One sunny Saturday morning en la Ciudad de México, before the orange smog hid the blue skies, I took a cab from my hotel to Coyoacán, formerly an ancient Aztec pueblo, now a charming *suburbio* of Mexico City. The yellow Volkswagen taxicab was brand-new and the driver winced when I slammed the door shut. Because of this, we drove in silence down Avenida Miguel Angel Quevedo and eventually came to a slow stop at an intersection, surrounded by a horde of other smog spewing vehicles.

I silently looked over to the shady sidewalk. In hindsight it was more of a strong urge, expecting to find something. My eyes climbed up some stairs to a high dark volcanic rock wall that resembled a pyramid. Atop sat a man with his back to the street. Instantly I recognized him. It was my father. His shock of white hair combed back, the peculiar shape of his head, smaller at the top, his ears showing, his dark horn rimmed eyeglasses barely visible. He wore a blue coat with a western cut. Friends always said he bore a striking resemblance to Spencer Tracy, with an Indian nose, steel-blue eyes and the white hair. My father had inherited the blonde traits from our grandmother, a petite, blue-eyed blonde woman of supposed French descent. But Santos Zapata de Burciaga had been very Mexicana with a long dark skirt and a shawl wrapped around her head and shoulders.

I sat in the cab amazed and mesmerized. I had not seen my father in such a long time. The feelings I'd left as a child returned: comfort, strength, a desire to run up to him in an embrace to kiss him. As a child he would have lifted me up in his strong muscled arms and rough calloused hands. I enjoyed seeing him peacefully resting on the cool black rock. But I was not going to disturb him for I knew things could never be the same between us.

The traffic light changed to green and the taxi gently and slowly pulled away. He heard the many cars pulling away behind him and he slowly turned his head to see. I looked away and immediately hid. I didn't want to see him anymore and I didn't want him to see me. He had begun to turn his head as if he knew I was there. The taxi went into second gear, third and we drove away. I hadn't seen my father since he died, 25 September 1986.

The surrealism of Mexico haunts me everytime I go back. As a child growing up in El Paso and crossing to Juarez every day I never noticed it. Today I think, maybe this is the surrealistic country and Mexico is the realistic one. Mexico is closer to an ancient culture and the reality of death. All my relatives, dead and alive, are scattered throughout Mexico. While here the culture feigns youth and life.

But in Mexico I recall the wakes of aunts and uncles; caskets filling the middle of an adobe living room or bedroom filled with the smell of burning candle wax. Women wrapped in shawls mumbled *Novenas, Letanias, Ave Marías* and *Padre Nuestros* while in the next room the hushed voices of *compadres* drank mezcal and traded gossip about the deceased.

One of the last times I saw my father was in an El Paso hospital. He had already suffered a stroke and could not communicate. The hospital overlooked the edge of the vast Mexican desert from the Río Bravo that glistened like a silver ribbon in the landscape. He had finally succumbed in his furious struggle against old age and infirmity. His one reminder to us was always, *"No te hagas viejo,"*—Don't grow old. And now he had resigned himself to the inevitable. He no longer had to be strapped to the hospital bed.

That late afternoon, Clete, my Irish-American *cuñado,* and I took him outside from his hospital room in a wheel chair. My *cuñado* offered my non-smoking father a cigarette. My father smiled. He could no longer laugh. We passed a *gobernador* tree. Clete cut a leafy branch with its unique desert smell and placed it in my father's hand. He gently held it, looked at the branch and raised it up to smell the desert. His eyes looked up to where the sun had just set and then turned to the rocky dark brown hills of his other country, a land he had known so well. His eyes became intense and then relaxed to the memories of a much earlier time. He couldn't speak, his lips were pursed, but his eyes said it all, traveling through his youth. *No te hagas viejo!* The Mexican revolution, riding the rails, dances, compadres, his father and his *vida* as a father. He had seen his *tierra* and he was at peace, the *sol* had already set. It would soon get dark so we took him back. That was the last time I saw him, I think.

BIRTH AND DEATH OF A MURAL

It was a magnificent and monumental mural that measured 150 feet long by 22 feet high. Nothing short of breathless, its beauty was primarily due to Gilberto Romero Rodriguez, a master muralist from Mexico, but it affected me more than any other work of art.

Titled *Danzas Mexicanas,* it depicted four regional folkloric dances from Mexico: the Jarocho dance from Veracruz, the Jarabe Tapatio from Jalisco; the Viejito Dance from

Michoacán and the Yaqui Deer Dance from Sonora. It was located in a downtown parking lot of a Great Western Savings Bank in Redwood City, California.

The story behind it is not unlike that of so many other murals. The giant wall had first come to my attention in 1975. A woman from the Redwood City Arts Commission had inquired about the possibility of my painting a mural on that wall. The Bicentennial was one year away and the commission wanted to commemorate the country's 200th birthday with murals.

We visited the wall. It was rough, the splattered concrete had been painted a few times. Cracks from the roof to the ground had been repaired with tar. First the wall had to be sandblasted and then we would have to find a paint that would adhere to tar.

One of the natural first questions was how much the job paid? The woman was momentarily startled but immediately gained her composure to answer, "Why no! There's no pay! This is strictly voluntary. But," she smiled, "we will pay you for the paint and brushes." Generous though she was, I thanked her and wished her well in her search. What I needed was a job.

Two years later I was again approached to paint a mural, this time by a Multicultural Arts Council. Would I be interested in being proposed for a California Arts Council grant to do three murals? "Sure!" I had nothing to lose. Art grants are like playing the lottery. To my surprise, It was funded and in 1978 I began work on the three murals. One was painted in a grade school. Tiny little kids drew their fish, whales, trees, suns, flowers, cats and dogs. I put them all together in a designed mural and the little kids filled the forms with color. After their painting sessions, I would go back to turn a blob into a fish or a flower.

The next mural, the most satisfying, was in a middle school. The kids were in the sixth grade, totally uninhibited, but took directions well. The mural in the gym was about flying saucers and martians.

The third was to be located in a visible downtown location and naturally I was attracted to that one wall 150 feet by 22 feet. By this time I was working as an arts administrator for the San Mateo County Arts Council. Nationally, unemployment had continued to soar and a Comprehensive Employment Training Act (CETA) was enacted by Congress. Similar to the Works Public Administration (WPA) during the depression, artists were put on the San Mateo County Arts Council payroll. I wasn't a CETA employee but was assigned a team of six CETA artists. They would help me paint a mural that was way bigger than I could have handled otherwise.

I researched the Mexican dances, photographs and pictures of dancers and their costumes. Then with the help of Chuy Campusano, a San Francisco muralist, we drew the long mural design. The research and drawing took approximately nine months.

We acquired scaffolding on wheels that reached eighteen feet high, and the wall was sandblasted. We found a special silver paint that would adhere to the tar which covered the cracks, allowing it to expand and contract with weather changes. After painting the entire 3,300 square foot wall we waited a week. At night we projected the design onto the wall with an old World War II overhead projector.

We began painting our design with Politec, specially developed acrylic mural paints from Mexico. A few days into the painting, it rained. After the rain, the warm sun dried the moisture and we returned to work. But the paint had begun to bubble. It had failed to adhere. I pinched the bubble and easily tore the paint off for a foot or more. Behind the piece of torn paint was the shiny silver paint. The ensuing nightmare came upon realizing that we would not only have to rip, tear and scrape all that we had painted, little as it was, but scrape the entire wall as well. The silver undercoat paint was not going to work. At the same time, the CETA artists were taken away from me to start on another project. I was left by myself. I had no other recourse than to call friends, Bernice Zamora, a poet, and her daughters, my *comadre* Emilia and others.

I borrowed electric drills and fitted them with rotating steel brushes. I also bought steel hand brushes. In a matter of three weeks we scraped away what we had painted, and what little remained dried so hard that it didn't cause a problem.

At the same time, I heard of a Mexican artist in San Francisco who was looking for work. His name was Gilberto Romero Rodriguez and he was helping Chuy Campusano, paint a mural in Daly City. I went to talk to him. He silently listened as he painted a blonde cheerleader in the mural.

After hearing the story, we set a time to go see what had become a nightmare.We studied the wall, made some tests with different paints, including a gesso paint over the silver surface. We waited two weeks that included a couple of rains and then, satisfied with the results, we painted the whole wall white.

One night we returned to reproject and draw the figures on the wall. Using an overhead projector from street level towards a twenty-two-foot wall caused a slight distortion. The figures would be top heavy. It was a good disfiguration. Once painted, mural observers from street level would see a normal figure. This was something Michelangelo had figured out centuries before. His sculpture of David is top heavy so that people at ground level will not see a distorted figure.

Thus we began the task of painting the mural and continued to do so for the next nine months. The pay was minimal, eight hundred dollars a month, and I was now splitting it with Gilberto. To help him, we provided room and board.

The mural was monumental not only in size but in the political, social and cultural repercussions that it could have. It was also a pleasant learning experience. Gilberto was the master. I became his apprentice. As a dedicated and serious muralist, he was thorough and taught me all he knew about murals. We didn't always apply the paint in the normal fashion. Because the wall was rough concrete we jabbed the brush into the wall with paint to cover the little holes and crevices. Only then would we paint lines and strokes. Eventually the mural began to take on its own life.

But all during this time, we had experienced one problem after another. After offering CETA helpers, the County Arts Council had taken them away. We had trouble collecting our small paychecks or getting reimbursed for the paints. The Director of the Multicultural Arts Center was too busy running his full-time job.

My last talk with him was a week before the inauguration of the mural. It was an argument over something I no longer remember. But I do remember he walked away from the argument and left me standing there. I was still trying to get reimbursed, to get paid and to also find a place downtown where we would be able to exhibit our easel work.

Cooperation was totally absent. While we were paid a minimal salary, the mural was being sponsored by a long list of organizations taking credit: not only the California Arts Council, but also the Multicultural Arts Council, the San Mateo County Arts Council, Cañada College, the Redwood City Merchants Association, and the Redwood City Chamber of Commerce. To say we were angry is an understatement, but meanwhile the mural looked gloriously beautiful and happy. The pleased sponsors were beginning to take more credit than they deserved.

The invitations for the dedication came out. A full-color detail of one of the dances graced the cover of the invitation and inside was a complete listing of the sponsors' names. But nowhere were the names Gilberto Romero Rodriguez and José Antonio Burciaga. Eventually the names were typed on stickers and added.

On our own we contacted the tenants of an empty Christian Science Reading Room that would soon open. They graciously allowed us to exhibit our work on that Sunday.

Saturday morning, the day before the mural dedication I proposed to Gilberto: "I'm going to get up there and talk about the use, abuse and exploitation of artists."

"Why don't we throw paint on it?" Gilberto countered.

I looked at him, trying to comprehend what he had just said. He was dead serious. It seemed reckless and easy for him. Gilberto was single and away from his family. I was married, with children and people to answer to. Some of the mural's sponsors were good people who had invested their time and faith.

"We get three bottles and fill each of them with the primary colors, red, blue and yellow."

I thought it would be the opposite of the creative process. It would be akin to destroying or killing. I hesitated, but instantly knew there was no way out of this alternative. My little angry speech would never have the impact of a visual aid.

"Let's talk to others about this," I suggested.

That night we attended a Chicano writers gathering at Stanford University. We presented our proposed protest but they couldn't bring themselves to either support or condemn it. I was convinced that the next day, with a clear head, we would have the courage to do something that might be totally condemned.

The next day, 25 February 1978, was a cold and cloudy Sunday. I awoke dreading what we had to do, knowing we would have to go through with our protest. Cecilia asked, "Are you going through with the protest?" Once I answered her, I would follow that course.

"Yes." I responded.

That morning I took three little Gerbers baby food jars and filled each one with a different color. In one I poured red, in a second jar I poured blue and in a third I poured white paint. Then I gave them to Gilberto who wanted to add an acrylic varnish extender that would make them more impervious than the paint on the mural. As I handed the three little jars to him he looked at them and said, "These aren't the primary colors." Somewhere in my mind I had misinterpreted the primary colors of red, blue and yellow for red white and blue.

"It's alright. We will use these," Gilberto answered. "Might be better."

So we decided on a strategy. We would be invited to the stage platform and I would read my speech in English and then introduce Gilberto who would say some words in Spanish. At the end of his speech he would pull out his jar with white paint. At the same time I would pull out my two bottles of red and blue paint. Together, and quickly, we would throw them against the mural wall. But we would throw them in areas removed from the dancing figures.

The dedication program began on a cloudy Sunday afternoon at 1 P.M.

A ballet folkloric dance group from the University of Sinaloa had been invited to perform as had an indigenous group of Aztec dancers. The mayor of Redwood City was there along with two or three San Mateo County Supervisors. Approximately five hundred people had come to witness the festive affair. Families came with kids. I winced as I thought of the kids I had taught to paint and respect murals. What the hell was I doing now? Eventually the woman mayor of Redwood City delivered her speech about "the fine mural and the two talented muralists." (Whose names she couldn't remember or didn't know how to pronounce.) "The mural is now a part of Redwood City for all to enjoy." The supervisors followed as did some of the organizers.

Then I was presented on stage by the director of the Multicultural Arts Council, the man with whom I had argued and fought incessantly. I kept my distance from him and as he left me on stage I called for Gilberto to join me. He was the one most responsible for the quality of the mural.

After a few introductory remarks about having gone through the creative process and the history of the wall, I recalled how someone had wanted me to paint a Bicentennial mural for free . . . "And so I would like to talk to you about the exploitation, use and abuse of artists . . ." I spoke to them not only as an artist but also as a former arts administrator for the San Mateo County Arts Council. I had left the arts administrative field after artist Manny Montoya had asked me, "What are you? An artist or an administrator?" I was caught between administrative decisions and the needs of the artists. As an arts administrator I had become aware of the amount of money given by the National Endowment for the Arts and the California Arts Council and how so little of it actually trickled down to the artists after paying for administration and the administrators.

In my mural dedication speech I detailed the many problems we had encountered with cooperation, reimbursements and our pay checks, small as they were. The audience fidgeted but mostly stood silent. I could feel the anger and embarrassment I was causing the organizers and the politicians as they stood silently by.

"Artists have power . . . and they should use it . . . Art is a process. This is the end product, this is the result of the process." I finished my speech, and then introduced Gilberto.

Gilberto walked forward stepped up to the microphone and described how the mural was not finished, it still needed a lot of work, we had not received the support and cooperation necessary to do a better job. His *maestros* in Mexico would be very disappointed in what had transpired.

As he drew his brief speech to an end I stepped from behind him to his side and put my hands in my jacket holding and feeling the cool glass jars with red and blue paint.

"I began this mural with white paint," said Gilberto, "and I finish it with white." He then pulled out his jar of white paint and hurled it at the wall, some twenty feet away.

At the same time, I pulled out my red paint and blue paint. I couldn't believe I was actually going through with this but I was flush with conviction more than anger. I threw one bottle of paint and ever so slowly I saw it hurling towards the wall and in an instant it crashed and in slow motion it opened up like a blue flower. Quickly I passed the other bottle to my right hand. I threw it with all my power and before my eyes, again in slow motion, a red flower blossomed upon the wall.

The audience was stunned. Some clapped, some whistled, some booed. Gilberto and I both jumped off the front of the stage, mingled into the crowd amid more cheers then jeers and then walked to the Christian Science Reading Room where our exhibit was located. On the way, a few people congratulated us.

Some people were splattered with paint. We took full responsibility for their clothes yet no one wanted compensation. Except for one German tourist. Dressed in white, he now had a few red, white and blue dots. He was furious and shouted how we should be lined against the wall and executed. The police went around asking if anybody wanted to press charges against us. No one did, apparently the German tourist was not asked.

The director of the Multicultural Arts Council wanted to know if there was a way of cleaning the paint off. The stains were small. Each no more than two and a half feet in diameter. In a 3300 square foot mural they were mere specks but on that day they stood out in all their varnished brilliance. Years after I would take people to see the mural and they would never notice the stains. And I would never bring out the long painful story.

After the exhibition we returned home to toast with friends. Then the telegrams and calls began to arrive, congratualting us for taking such a stand. The next day the calls continued, this time from the press. I had invited the press to the dedication with the promise of a news story but all they had done was to notify the police. It now became obvious why the police had been tagging so close.

The next Thursday, *the San Francisco Chronicle's* art critic, Alfred Frankenstein, published my statement. The local papers, television and radio stations continued to call asking for interviews. It was an unnerving experience. One angry reporter wanted to make more of it than was there by suspecting misappropriation of funds. The San Mateo County Arts Council Director asked me to call them off. I did. There was no misappropriation of funds.

The controversy continued to flare around the Bay Area. "What right did artists have to inflict such a protest to a commissioned work of art?" Our response was multifaceted. The Multicultural Arts Council had failed to keep its word in the agreement. The artistic process sometimes changes from the original concept. The protest, the throwing of the paint was now part, parcel and history of the mural. It was not defacement, vandalism or destruction but an inevitable part of the artistic process.

For the next ten years, the mural graced that wall. The only graffiti to ever touch the mural occurred a few days after dedication. It was a vague comment on what artists can do compared to vandals. We painted over it and the mural remained clean until . . .

1 November 1988

Day of the Dead

Ten years after the dedication of the mural, I took a drive

through downtown Redwood City and detoured to take a look at the mural. I hadn't seen it in three months. Slightly faded by the sun, it was still holding well.

As I approached the wall I noticed that another building had been constructed and now covered the mural from two blocks away. But the closer I got to the wall, the more I realized the mural had been painted over. The wall was now blank, buried under a dull, lifeless beige. I was surprised and not surprised. I must have smiled at the irony of it all, here today, gone tomorrow. Nothing lasts forever. What gall, I thought. I went home, not knowing who to call or what to do. Gilberto had returned to Mexico. I would have to inform him.

Late that night I returned to the wall with three plastic bags of red, white and blue paint. The shops were closed, the downtown streets were empty. I drove into the parking lot, stepped out and slammed the three bags against their freshly painted beige wall.

The next day there was no reaction and a few days later there was a column in the paper about the mural no longer existing, with no comment on the paint splashes. Great Western Savings Bank had enlarged their building, landscaped the parking lot and received permission from the owner to paint over the mural. The Bank had supposedly called twenty-two times to find the muralists without success. Our names were on the mural's right hand bottom corner and mine in the telephone directory.

Three days after my initial attack on their beige wall I returned and splattered more red white and blue paint. But this time I called the news media and they came out and did a story about the mural that no longer was.

Murals are painted and erased daily. I don't have problems with their erasures if something else takes their place. I agree with San Francisco muralist Ray Patlán, "If artists paint about change, we should be willing to accept change." But in this case it was the obliteration and deletion of not only public art but a cultural statement. The sterile look of the bank had returned.

We had an arts lawyers advocacy organization but our case was slim. The Great Western Savings Bank was generous enough to give $3,000 to be split between a Mexican ballet folkloric dance troupe in the East Palo Alto community, Gilberto and myself.

When Gilberto received word, he was able to get more media coverage in Mexico about the incident. I sent him his money. He never returned, but someday I will hear from him again. All that is left of the mural are slides, pictures, clippings, and 8-mm footage that has been transferred to a video of young happy muralists painting and taking a break with a six pack of Dos Equis.

But in a bizarre way, our mural protest had become part of a process in which life and art were fused into one.

COLORES

Community organizer Daniela Gomez likes to tell the story about a group of Latino women from East Palo Alto who were encouraged to produce arts and crafts items for sale downtown. The items involved crocheting, and making little baskets with bright colorful flowers and ribbons.

The ladies appreciated their efforts but told them through an interpreter that the little baskets would not sell because the colors were too bright and gaudy for the home decor of Palo Alto residents. "You must use subtle pastel colors that will go with their decor."

The information was graciously interpreted. But the bewildered *Latinas* frowned, "Those are *colores de muertos,* colors for the dead."

In this country, rugs, towels, fabric and wallpaper with Southwestern Indian designs are hot and can be found in most department stores. But these items have gone through a "decolorization," "pastelization" process, or what Chicano poet Juan Felipe Herrera calls "amigoization." The colors have been muted for mainstream consumption.

Bright colors are not appreciated in western culture. Consider the cardiac arrest Western Culture had when the Sistine Chapel murals were cleaned. My God! Michelangelo had painted with bright colors. The muted colors of the Sistine Chapel had been nothing more than grime and smoke from centuries of candles, heat and moisture.

Prevalent as it is, color is one of the most complex and misunderstood subjects in the world. Its interpretation and psychology is culturally based and biased. If color were to be taught to children, adolescents and adults, would it make any difference in teaching culture and people appreciation?

Faber Birren, a world renowned color consultant explains, "It affects us emotionally, making things warm or cold, provocative or sympathetic, exciting or tranquil . . . Color is information . . . Until it reaches the brain, color does not exist."

Why are the colors of Chicano, Latino and American Indian and African American artists so much brighter than that of most other cultures? Many of us were taught Western Culture answers: primitivism, folklore, colorful, unrefined . . .. Had we been born in the East Coast, England or France, would we not be painting with softer pastel colors, toned down by gray cloudy skies, toned down by the surrounding vegetation that soaks the sunlight? The sun over Africa, Latin America, including the Southwest bounces from the mountains, the desert and back to the sky. The sun over these parts of the world burns brighter, stronger and hotter not only on the land but is also reflected in their culture. What some label passionate.

I never thought beyond this explanation until I heard musician Carlos Santana speak about color. "Color has sound!" he exclaimed. I had never seriously considered the use of color as sound.

I immediately visualized and heard the colors musicians played: Mariachis! Rock n' Roll! Symphonies! Blues Bands! Salsa Bands! I could see the colors and not just listen to the notes in all their brilliant tone, hue and texture. "Singing the blues" is more than a metaphor. Dancing polkas is akin to polka dots. Music and color share a common vocabulary with words such as "harmony" and "tone."

I began to repeat Santana's words until a puzzled young student quietly asked, "How can you hear colors?" First, psychologically, but there is also a scientific answer, color is like sound, a vibratory phenomenon. Each color is like a musical note. Red, at one end of the spectrum, has the lowest frequency (number of vibrations per second) and the longest wave length. It is analogous to a deep sound of low pitch. The frequency increases as it passes through the other colors of the spectrum.

In addition, our senses are interdependent on one another. My ears are dependent on my eyes and vice versa. There was a man in New York who regained his eyesight after fifty-some years. Rather than a joyous continuation to his life, the man was thrown into confusing despair. He found out how dependent he had been of his other senses and now sight had only served to confuse him. The many colors in a supermarket almost terrorized him. Who can taste without the use of the olfactory senses? You need your nose to taste food.

"*Our senses serve the mind. Our mind is not intuitive. Natural beauty comes through the senses and delights the mind. Conscious awareness. A beautiful color washes the eye. The form is apprehended in the sensible. Rejoice without labor or without discussion.*"—anonymous.

Colors emit expressions and fit into patterns, sequences, sculptures, sounds, lyrical impulses, spiritual doubts or convictions, and dimly realized truths. Through color one can create love, joy, sadness, pity and pain. Emotions are universal, only the colors in their harmony, textures, tones and sounds are different.

The Eskimos have over a hundred words for snow and, different kinds of white. People who live in the desert have a wide variety of terms for yellow and brown.

Before thinking of "body painting" as a cultural trait of "less developed civilizations" consider the cosmetic industry in the "developed countries," to say nothing of tattoos and sun bathing.

One book on color explains how some early languages contain no color names and uses the Bible as an example, " . . . although there are over four hundred references to the sky or heaven, the color blue is not named." In many cultures, the term "sky" or "heaven" is enough to conjure the color blue.

American Indians attributed certain colors to each of the four directions. Red for the direction from which the sun is born every day. Black or blue for where the night comes, or goes. White for the cold north. Yellow for the south where the weather is milder.

Some time ago I read a poem by an American Indian woman about the cold white snow melting and how it would soon be Spring and all the colors would visit again.

Likewise, the United Farm Workers anthem is De Colores, about how the fields dress in colors in the springtime: *De colores se visten los campos en la primavera . . . Y por eso los grandes amores de muchos colores me gustan a mi*—And that is why I like great loves in many colors.

But these "nice and lovely" thoughts have no serious place in the curriculum of most schools. In a consumer culture, the popular media critics will brand these words as nothing more than entertainment or propaganda. Color is found in the aesthetic disciplines of music, art, dance and drama, the first subjects to go when schools are financially strapped, without realizing that aesthetics is tied to ethics and science. Color is not only music, it is also light and it is truth.

BILINGUAL COGNATES

Bilingual Love Poem

Your sonrisa is a sunrise
that was reaped from your smile
sowed from a semilla
into the sol of your soul
with an ardent pasión,
passion ardiente,
sizzling in a mar de amar
where more is amor,
in a sea of sí
filled with the sal of salt
in the saliva of the saliva
that gives sed but is never sad.

Two tongues that come together
is not a French kiss
but bilingual love.

A cognate is a word related to another through derivation, borrowing or descent. From one language to another, I suppose they become bilingual cognates if not bloopers. Like in the poem above, there are Spanish and English words that look alike or sound alike:

—Vincent Price has been known as "beans

and rice" or vice versa.

—El Benny Lechero was actually a short serial movie character in the fifties known as "The Vanishing Shadow."

— Somewhere in the Southwest there was a teacher who thought his Chicano kids were calling him "Cool Arrow" when in reality they were calling him a *"culero,"* an insult.

—Two Chicanos were dining at a fashionable restaurant and one of them says to the other, "This is the best *gabacho (gazpacho)* soup I've ever tasted.

—My mother once called her comadre and her German born husband answered. "Lucina is not in," he said in perfect Spanish, "she is out buying *'grocerías.'"* (*Grocerías* are coarse, vulgar statements and acts.)

—One morning our friend Muggins called and my Mother answered. Trying to be courteous, he asked my Mother in Spanish how she was born instead of how she had awakened: *"Buenos dias, Señora, ¿Como nació?"* instead of *"¿Como amaneció?"*

Some are not necessarily cognates but the mental mistranslations sometime result in funny situations. My friend Rana has forever confused his Spanish with his English. As a high schooler, he was dazzled by a beautiful young woman and greeted her with "How are you going?" from *"¿Como te va?"* Even in English he had trouble. Lone Star Beer became Long Star, humble became noble, and misconstrew became misconstrue. In the context of a serious conversation the result is laughter.

Jokes abound about Latinos who come to this country

and read English signs in Spanish. Back when Cokes were only a dime, a Mexicano put a ten cent coin in the machine but did not receive a bottle of Coke. He waited, hit it and nothing. Finally he read just above the coin slot where it said "Dime" (which translates to "tell me" in Spanish}. So he bent down to the slot and whispered into it, *"Dame una Coca Cola."*

We have all seen real estate signs that say "For Sale, No Lease."A newly arrived immigrant looking for housing, read the sign and kicked the door open. If you read that in Spanish and run the first two words together it reads, "force it, it's alright."

Introducing someone in Spanish is not the same as introducing someone in English. *Introducir* in Spanish means to put in, to infiltrate. The correct term is *presentar.* Yet *introducir* is used so often that people don't even catch it. Many bilingual cognates have returned to Mexico to become part of what is known as Mexican caló. *Chansa* comes from chance, for *oportunidades. Trakes* for tracks, *mechas* for matches, *chutear* for shooting, *raides* from rides. Mexican film actor Tin Tan and singer Juan Gabriel have been very influential in "introducing" Chicano terms to Mexico.

Most of the Spanish terminology for baseball comes from the English. *Ni ketcha, ni pitcha, ni deja batear* is a well known proverb for someone who won't do anything and won't let anyone else do anything—He/she won't catch, doesn't pitch and won't let anyone bat.

One of my favorite anecdotes is the one about my good

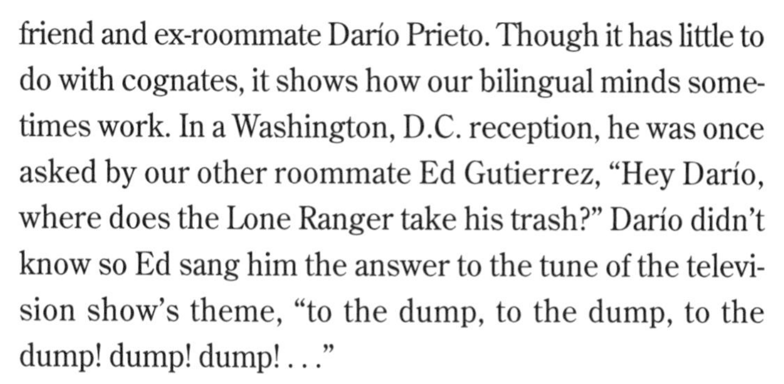

friend and ex-roommate Darío Prieto. Though it has little to do with cognates, it shows how our bilingual minds sometimes work. In a Washington, D.C. reception, he was once asked by our other roommate Ed Gutierrez, "Hey Darío, where does the Lone Ranger take his trash?" Darío didn't know so Ed sang him the answer to the tune of the television show's theme, "to the dump, to the dump, to the dump! dump! dump! . . ."

Darío laughed heartily and then went to ask a couple the same question. But Darío always had to polish his English. He cleared his throat, something he always did, and asked, "Where does the Lone Ranger dispose of his debris?" The couple didn't know, so Darío sang the answer, "Ta-da-da, ta-da-da, ta-da-da,da,da . . ." The couple just stared at him.

FROM COMEDY FIESTA TO CULTURE CLASH

Should you ever be possessed with an overwhelming urge to be a comedian because you have an overproductive humor gland that makes your family and friends break into convulsions of laughter whenever you speak, try yourself out on amateur night at your local comedy club.

That's what I did even though I wasn't the funny one in my family. My father was far more humorous in his daily life. My earliest memory of his humor was when he was interned in a hospital with second-degree burns and a broken right arm. My father read everything at a full arm's length but this time his arm was set in plaster at 45 degrees. Trying to read a note in his right hand, he deadpanned, "I don't need glasses; what I need is a longer arm." His hospital roommate erupted into laughter and split his abdominal stitches. My father was reprimanded and moved to another room.

My brother Efraín is also funnier than me. He can still get his graying buddies to laugh nonstop, one crack after another. He took his humor seriously. As a kid, Efraín would paste cartoons from *Colliers, Saturday Evening Post, Look* and other now deceased publications unto a scrapbook.

I was the serious and shy one. The first times I made anyone laugh was by accident. Or maybe it was to deflect attention away from myself. If I became the center of attention with no way of escaping, I would use words to detract their eyes away from me. Humor would dissolve the seriousness of their looks. It was unconscious for me in the beginning.

But I soon realized the power of humor to offset, convince and lighten conversations that sometimes bogged down or became myopic. I listened and studied my father and brother Efraín. We visited the old library in downtown and checked out all the "Best Cartoon" of the year anthologies.

In the process we also discovered books about the birds and the bees— that's what ¡SEX EDUCATION! used to be called. The library became our Lenten sanctuary (we called it that because during Lent we weren't suppose to go to movies or enjoy ourselves too much) where we laughed and learned about life, about sex and humor. What else was there to do during Lent or on sizzling 114 degree summer days before "air conditioning" was invented. There is no statue in El Paso, honoring the person who invented air conditioning. After "air conditioning" arrived the library became even more inviting, except for the movie theaters that advertised air conditioning with painted icicles, igloos and penguins. But it seemed like it was always Lent, school work or without the necessary nine cents for a movie.

In all that reading I also discovered that to find humor in a situation, one had to relax and leave the mind open to any and everything, and then to associate it to some off-the-wall item. Putting incongruous things together, things that don't necessarily go together can be funny. Mexican culture and Anglo- American culture have as many incongruities between them as commonalties.

But it has to be natural humor, it can't be forced. Some comedians force their humor. It has to come easily, out of left field, when you least expect it, dressed like you have never seen it before.

Canned laughter doesn't help. It is about as farcical as television wrestling. There was a recent, not-very-funny comedy show made for cable television. The audience was sitting up straight without moving but the audio was filled with roaring laughter. Live late-night humor is much more genuine, and funnier.

But getting back to my story, it was our father's influence, that made us admire and respect humor as a great antidote and a wonderful way to see and appreciate things. Humor gives insight into this crazy world, and how seriously or outrageously we take ourselves. I would ask my father if he had seen my brother. He would stop and stick his hands in his pockets, as if looking for a little piece of paper, while I waited patiently. He would then answer, *No está aquí.* Then there were the Mexican jokes, daily or weekly, we heard the latest from our aunts, uncles and cousins in Juarez. Our parents took us to the latest Cantinflas films. Anglo-American humor just wasn't as funny to us. Mexican humor can be more direct, raw and provoking.

Humor offers a way to get out of serious situations. There is a lot of humor to be found in the irony of living between and within two cultures, between and within two political ideologies, between two countries, two languages. In a Christmas card drawing, the three wisemen become three Mexican cowboys on horseback, cutting through a chain link barbed wire fence. Former Secretary of State Henry Kissinger became Enrique Kissinger, "The Greatest Matador North of the Border" when he chaired a committee of American politicos sent to study Central American issues. Dressed as a fat matador, Kissinger holds a cape and pistol to a charging bull.

Poetry, for the most part has always been considered a sedate and serious art form. Literary decorum requires it have a serious attention span. When the Chicano literary movement exploded, much of our poetry was angry, didactic, painful, melodramatic, too academic or too Anglo-American influenced. Very few injected humor into their poetry. The laughter amused many audiences. However, humor was never taken seriously.

Having discovered the power of humor, I began performing my poetry. In 1974 after thinking about it for more than four years, I wrote Letanía en Calo, a religious church litany utilizing Caló, the Chicano dialect. It was funny to most, but a few found it profoundly blasphemous. Some walked out on my presentations. This poetic litany required a response from the audience, *Ruega por Nosotros* (pray for us), and *Líbranos Señorr* (liberate us, oh Lord). I dressed as a priest, wearing a black suit with a black shirt worn backwards and a white collar showing in the front. Some thought I was a radical priest. Nuns and priests would walk up, take note of my outfit and walk away, embarrassed that they had been taken in.

Back in 1975, between a matinee and a night performance, I strolled through downtown San José dressed as a priest carrying a sack lunch. I did a lot of head bowing on my way to a park bench. Everybody greets priests with bows of the head. At the park bench I heard one confession, listened to the life story of a homeless person, and counseled one woman: "Yes," I advised her, "If your sister does not baptize her child, by all means you have the moral obligation to secretly baptize the child." It was valid. I had learned this from twelve years of catholic education. But I didn't like being a public priest.

That same year I performed a poem entitled"Berta

Crocker's Bicentennial Recipe" while dressed with an apron in the middle of a kitchen set on television. As I recited the poem, I took out a knife, slashed into a cake mix box that contained two eggs, and three plastic bags, one red, one white, and one blue. Mixing those flag colors with two huevos in a bowl resulted in a beautiful brown cake mix. I poured the mix into a cake mold and put it in the oven for two hundred years. I let it rise and propagate and then I pulled out a beautiful chocolate cake.

In November of 1983 Rene Yañez, San Francisco artist and gallery curator invited me to join Richard Montoya, Monica Palacios and Marga Gomez to form a Comedy Fiesta for Cinco de Mayo 1984. Marga Gomez is a New Yorican of a Puerto Rican mother and Cuban father. Monica Palacios, is a Chicana but claims she was born in San José and left when she found out.

Yañez had been doing art performances with Richard Montoya, a young actor, and son of José Montoya. José was another very funny bato, and the grandfather of Chicano poetry.

Rather than going on stage cold turkey with Comedy Fiesta, I decided to try out my material at a San Francisco comedy club called the Valencia Rose. The name was poignantly fitting for the now defunct gay comedy club. Like a bleeding rose, the effects of AIDS were beginning to be felt. Located in San Francisco's Mission District, it was the only place where amateur Chicano/Latino comedians, gay or straight, could try out their material. Marga Gomez and Monica Palacios were regulars and at their suggestion

I decided to go one Tuesday night.

I was a little nervous driving to the club; by the time I arrived there I was catatonic, in total shock. I had forgotten what I was there for. I clearly remember the sensations: shallow breathing, a dry mouth, I frantically wanted to run in panic. What had possessed me? What kind of predicament had I now put myself in? No one knew except Cecilia and Monica Palacios, who arranged for me to go on stage. I was there by myself. If I was really funny, even total strangers would laugh at my humor.

I fidgeted nervously in the dark empty backstage. A small audience laughed and applauded the one or two other comedians. When my turn came, my legs grudgingly and nervously strode on stage while my mind was frantically running the other way.

There was no way I was going to be able to remember all my jokes. Memorization has never been a strength and in front of an audience my mind had been known to go blank. I decided to walk on stage like a lecturing professor and read from a lectern on the Official English Movement which was in full conservative vogue at that time:

"How far will the Official English Movement go?" I asked the audience. "Will they want me to change my name to Joseph Anthony, Big Headed? (That is what it translates to in the Basque language) I have a friend named Nieves Palomares. Will they change her name to "Ice Cream Pigeon House"? What will they change my friend Facundo's name to? I guess they will have to deport him since they won't know the translation. Hilarious material, I thought. But only one person was politely laughing and she was being drowned out by silence.

"If they are going to declare English the official language, perhaps they should also change the Spanish names of all the towns and cities as well. For instance, there's a little island in the San Francisco Bay called Yerba Buena. They would have to change that to Good Grass or Good Weed. There's a town called Los Baños. That would change to The Bathrooms, California. Manteca would become Lard, California and Atascadero would become Mud Puddle."

Funny! I should have had them rolling on the concrete floor the way I had done at other readings but the audience was totally quiet except for the one older woman laughing more and more as time went on. This woman at the back of the audience was beginning to grate on my nerves. Everyone else was totally silent and with lights glaring on me I couldn't tell if they were asleep, bored or angry. Perhaps they had been paid not to laugh.

"Tornillo, Texas would be changed to Screw, Texas," I continued. "And there are two towns named Socorro: Socorro, New Mexico and Socorro, Texas. One would be changed to Help I and the other Help II. If you help one, you gotta help the other too."

The laughing woman was overdoing it. She was now roaring dementedly while everyone else sat stone-faced. Couldn't she see that no one else was laughing? Was she crazy or what? "Get her out of here!" I wanted to yell. "She's ruining my debut, my act, my presentation. But no, she was just beginning. Death had to be a lot more humane than this. I was mortified. My mind was telling my body to run but my body just stood there, taking one lash of silence after another. The woman was embarrassing me. She was laughing at me.

I ended to very polite applause except for the crazy woman that continued to laugh. I was so relieved my body wanted to crawl but there was nothing it could crawl under. It went out into the hallway and headed straight for the doorway. My mind was disassociating itself from my body.

The cool Bay Area night air was refreshing to my red hot face. But I felt immediate relief, knowing I was not that funny and that I would not fit into the Chicano/Latino comedy troupe called Comedy Fiesta. I had honestly tried and honestly failed.

After my disastrous debut I could hardly wait to call Rene "I can't do it. I'm not as funny as I thought. It didn't work you know . . .." But he just didn't accept it. "You just need a little work, a little coaching . . .You'll do alright." He had the whole lineup: There was the young brash Richard Montoya born in a Sacramento Mall with one eye blue and the other gray, claiming to be part Jewish; Marga Gomez, a Cuban-Puerto Rican New Yorker; Monica Palacios, a San José Chicana and myself.

In the Mission District was another young talented artist and actor of Salvadoran descent named Herbert Siguenza. Upon learning of this venture, he asked Rene for an audition, and the benevolent godfather nodded, Sí. Then Herbert invited another young rap singer named Ricardo

Salinas, originally from El Salvador. Slic Ric came to one of our meetings and auditioned with an impressive and original Chicano rap. The group grew to dos mujeres and cuatro machos. We called ourselves Comedy Fiesta.

After rehearsals and much patience, we debuted on Cinco de Mayo, 1984 as "Comedy Fiesta." We advertised it as "The Only *Pinchi* Chicano/Latino Comedy Troupe in the Universe."

One hour before curtain time there was already a big line of people. Unfortunately, it turned out to be a line of people boarding a bus. Nonetheless the show did sellout that night, the next night and the next weekend . . .

I discarded my attempts at memorization and came on stage with visual aids, a map of the United States and a Mexican bag of props. Dressed like a Mexican flea market merchant, I explained I had just come from the flea market "where I had sold a few things and picked up a few things." With this said, I scratched myself. I carried a machete as a pointer and a colorful Mexican bag with an assortment of Mexicano and Chicano *yonque* items: A six pack of votive candles, each one dedicated to a particular saint; San Judas Tadeo, patron saint of the impossible *pendejos* which I would light for Ronald Reagan . . . A pair of jumper cables, "Every Chicano should have a set, especially if overweight." Then I would jump rope with the cables. A bottle of Oil of Olay became bullfighters' sun tan lotion. A *tostada* with the miraculous apparition of Christ became Taco Jesus. Inside the big colorful bag I carried a greasy bag with my lunch: a burrito on a stick, a bottle of Dos Equis beer and tostadas with written proverbs from my mother. Besides my lunch, I also carried jalapeños, chiles serranos, New Mexico chile, Anaheim, different types of bananas, and pork rinds. I explained their humorous differences and shared them with the audience. I carried fresh packs of tortillas and tossed them out to the audience as the first frisbees.

The first performance took place in the small Galeria de la Raza exhibit area in the San Francisco Mission District. The audience sat on a variety of chairs and benches. The backstage was a dead end small room with one tiny window for ventilation. Except for a few glitches and Richard Montoya taking more time than anyone else, Comedy Fiesta was rustic but an enjoyable hit. The next Sunday night was a sellout and the show was extended for the next two weekends.

Thus was born Comedy Fiesta. What was to have been a one time presentation was repeated again and again as we realized our success was too great to disband.

The name was changed to Culture Clash. We began to perform throughout the Bay Area and a following quickly formed. But other than the Valencia Rose in San Francisco and La Peña in Berkeley, we never performed in any comedy club. We found comedy clubs to be professionally cliquish at best and racist at worst. The owner of one comedy club in San José informed us that he did not want Mexican clientele in his club. What that left us with were alternative spaces such as closed bars, banquets, restaurants, high schools and universities.

Our first big break was performing at El Teatro Campesino at the invitation of Luis Valdez. The night was a standing-room-only sellout. To say I was terrified would be an understatement. But our performances were good enough to have earned high compliments from Luis Valdez and Frank Sarcoma, producer of public television's "Comedy Night," who advised us, "With a little bit of polish, you guys can go places."

Early Culture Clash consisted of six individuals, each with a different rountine or skit, which was tied to, or introduced the next. Marga Gomez was the most accomplished and experienced. Next came Monica Palacios who had worked with Marga and by herself. Herbert Siguenza was and continues to be a phenomenal impersonator of such diverse entertainers as Julio Iglesias, Michael Jackson, Al Pacino alias Tony Montana. Slic Ric Salinas had a special way with dancing, rap singing and a few impersonations. In the beginning it was Richard Montoya who tried the hardest, sometimes too hard, going out on a limb with humor that offended individual audience members or staying on stage too long. Our shows invariably ran three hours, sometimes more.

As a six-member troupe we lasted together for approximately two years. Then Marga and Monica decided to return to their own independent professional lives. The separation was amiable though it was highly influenced by insensitive material about women and gays.

A few of the conflicts were serious, bordering on funny. We performed in this one gallery where the backstage had no exit but a tiny window. Montoya's act went on for a full hour before I had to follow him. I was so angry, I quit after my presentation. With no door to leave through, I climbed through the tiny window in the back and jumped seven feet to the sidewalk.

It took an hour telephone conversation from the Godfather to convince me to return. Over the next year and a half we continued to perform throughout California, and then to San Antonio, Laredo, Connecticut and at the New York Joe Papp Latino Theater Festival. Richard, Slic Ric and Herbert became a trio and worked out skits among themselves while I developed my own routine. My humor appealed to the older and more Mexicano audiences, while the three guys appealed to younger mainstream Latinos. Rene had to drop off as producer.

As the trio took full control of the show and developed their own skits, I urged them to replace Marga and Monica but they were having too much fun and refused saying that there was no one else available. I finally realized that the twenty years between us was greater than I thought. Married, with a family and responsibilities, I had become a separate funny appendage.

Of all the art disciplines, none is more gratifying than to be on stage. The immediate audience response is seductive and stays with performers long after a show. The adrenaline continues to pump and it is easy to continue celebrating. Then one has to drive home and recuperate part of the next morning. By now I had overcome stage fright but was smoking and drinking too much before each show. One day I realized how useless it was and how much it was hurting and affecting my timing. I was pushing the limits of a kind of life filled with risk for my family, my writing and art. There were things more important than a career in comedy and so I bid farewell to the guys. Their reaction was one of sincere regret so they left the door open for me to return anytime. I appreciated their offer, and in fact did return as a fill-in at a Fresno show after Slic Ric was shot and almost killed.

Some people were surprised at my departure from Culture Clash. Luis Valdez teased that I might be considered the fifth Beatle. I knew Culture Clash would be successful the moment they set foot on L.A. stages but I couldn't see a future with them.

And, sure enough, Culture Clash went on to bigger things. Their stage shows, such as "Bowl of Beings," "The Mission" and "Carpa Clash" were ingenious and tight. Their stage performances are even better than their television work. Culture Clash is immensely popular with young people, high schoolers and college kids. They have appeared in films with Michael Douglas, Al Pacino, Andy Garcia and are filming a movie of their own. Marga Gomez has returned to preform with them on stage, and she is hilariously funny in her own career. (Since Culture Clash started with more women than men I miss that balance at times, though they're always hysterical.)

When introduced as a former member of Culture Clash young people find it hard to believe. Incredulous, they look at my gray hair, "You were with Culture Clash?" It wasn't that long ago.

Much of the credit for Culture Clash goes to Rene Yañez, an artist and curator who has created so many other Chicano art firsts, including humorous art exhibits, performance art, Day of the Dead Altars and Rooms for the Dead exhibits. Culture Clash's patience and fortitude is also to be admired. What Comedy Fiesta and the resulting Culture Clash did was to give a shot in the arm to a gone-stale Teatro Chicano. Culture Clash became the inspiration for many other Chicano/Latino comedy troupes such as Latins Anonymous, Chicano Secret Service, Los Illegals and The Alter Boys. And some continue to fly solo on wings of laughter.

Should you still be interested in becoming a comedian or forming your own comedy troupe, go for it. It is an inexpensive way to experience death, an out of body experience, life after death or at least you can practice dying.

Caution. Most teachers should not attempt to be funny in their classrooms. Not because they might lack a sense of humor, but because in the classroom setting it can be received defensively. It didn't work for me in the classroom and it didn't work for me the first time I tried out on amateur night as a lecturer, but I've gotten my share of laughs out of people, I guess, and I had some laughs myself.

DREAMS AND FLOWERS FOR MARGARITA

October, 1994

From time to time, my sister dreamed of events that would eventually happen. I wouldn't have called her a "psychic." That's too scientific a term for a natural phenomenon lying outside the sphere of physical science. I personally suspect she was visited by a strong spirit who fed her these dreams.

As a young girl, Margarita learned the virtue of silence about these dreams of the future. They were too eerie, too much like living in a dream.

"They're few and far between," she claimed. But I wondered if she wasn't suppressing them. Margarita never talked much about dreams.

The first time her clairvoyance was discovered our *mamá* started to tell Margarita, "Did you know that . . .?" Margarita interrupted, "¡No me diga! Ramón married Lourdes." The marriage between two family friends, Ramón, divorced, and Lourdes, an ex-nun, had caught everyone by surprise, everyone but Margarita, who had dreamed it.

When our mother died in 1985, Toño, my son, had a dream about his grandmother. Nine years later, the dream still haunts me. I called Margarita, hoping that by retelling the dream I could break his spell.

"The day after our mother died, Toño dreamed he had been in a car accident and gone to heaven where he had explained the details of the crash to Grammy. Now that Toño is driving, the dream haunts me more," I said over the phone.

"It's very natural," Margie empathized, "to have these fears about our children. My biggest fear is dying and leaving Oscar and Aaron, especially Aaron. The other day, he asked if I would be here to dance with him at his graduation."

After that conversation, I proposed to God, that if He wanted to take anybody from this family He should take me.

Something similar had happened in our family once before. Our aunt, Tía Nati, short for Natividad, was a nun with the Sisters of Charity in an El Paso convent. Unlike my blonde, blue-eyed father, Tía Nati had a rich brown face with striking Indian features. One day, she visited our father who was deathly ill. The next day she called to say she was praying for her brother and had offered her life to God in exchange for our father's life. "I'm a *monja, sola en un convento.* I have no family. Your father has a big family." Gradually, our father's health returned to normal. But gradually, my Tía's health deteriorated and before long she passed away.

Thursday
15 December 1994
Menlo Park, California

I awoke twice last night, at 3:00 and at 5:45. At 6:30 I decided to get up. I had the beginnings of a cold and felt restless. But before getting up, as I lay in bed with my hands on my stomach I felt something hard, a lump on the left side of my stomach just beneath my ribs. It was about the size and hardness of a *calabaza,* a zucchini. But I couldn't remember swallowing a whole squash the night before. I picked up my pajamas and discovered the unevenness on the left side of my stomach. I had never noticed this, though it was too large to miss.

I touched it, pressed it, and looked down at it again as I lay there, more puzzled than concerned, thinking to myself, "Is it natural? No! it's not natural." But I also thought, "Maybe *it is* natural. Were I to go see my doctor she might explain something I had never noticed before in my 54 years. And I would feel like both relieved and stupid. I hoped."

I got out of bed, stood straight and looked down for the lump that had now disappeared into a normal looking stomach. It was gone, just like that. I took a shower, the warm water waking up my body, soaking it, starting the day fresh, feeling clean, a daily ritual of our kingdom come, our daily resurrection from the death of night sleep. If the lump was serious . . .well, as long as I can take a shower the day I die, I will die happy.

At a quarter past seven, Toño still hadn't gotten up. I knocked on his locked door. There was no answer so I banged on the door with my fist. I lost it. He came out, half asleep. I bawled him out. He looked at me with half- closed eyes and after a minute of yelling at him, I walked away.

Toño, Rebeca and I were temporarily living in Menlo Park. After Toño's high school graduation we would move a couple of hours south to Monterey, where their mother Cecilia lived and worked.

That morning, I fiddled around in my art studio and at 8:25 I called the Stanford Mid-Peninsula Health Clinic. Their answering service asked that I call back in a few minutes when they opened.

I called back and asked for Doctor Marioka. They put me on hold. An eternal moment passed and then it dawned on me that I better leave—I had to be at San Lorenzo High School in an hour and I still had to buy some 35mm film. (I had a contract to teach art and literature in three special limited-English-proficiency classes in three high schools.)

What a racket! If you're sick and you want to see the doctor, you have to make an appointment and basically have a whole lot of time on your hands. Appointments can only be made during hours that are convenient to them.

I take off to San Lorenzo, cross the San Francisco Bay on the San Mateo Bridge. It's a glorious day, the sky is blue. Yesterday was miserable, wet with sloppy rain, the pavement reflecting the gray skies.

I think of the lump and try to feel it as I drive. My hand goes deep into my stomach and I feel something there. It worries me about as much as it puzzles me. I'm a bit scared, but not much. There's always an explanation for everything. But I seriously think it's a tumor. And I do think of cancer. "God, I hope not! I don't think so!" I say to myself. Cancer is an ugly word, an ugly disease. Most of the time it's terminal. I can't remember anybody beating cancer. People linger with this. And I have so much to do.

At San Lorenzo High School I was only going to pick-up a couple of self-portraits by two students and then excuse myself. I wasn't up to teaching class that day, but the students were eager to go ahead with the project I had assigned so I stayed.

The class made up of eighteen Chicano and Mexicano students was in Spanish. They spoke some English but were much more proficient in Spanish. Shannon Freeland, their teacher, a beautiful young woman who spoke Spanish very well, was kind and attentive.

The assignment was for each student to draw and write their autobiographical portrait together. First, I took slide portraits of each student. At the next class we projected each portrait onto a large sheet of drawing paper. With a light number #3 pencil, I had them outline their hair, faces, features, hair, eyelashes, lips and even shadows. Then each student wrote spontaneously about their hair, noses, ears or anything about their lives, whatever came to their minds. I showed them autobiographical portraits of other students and one I had done of myself. The project is very effective because they use the intuitive, right side of their mind to write while they are filling the forms. They took to the project brimming with curiosity.

That day they were well into working and their portraits were taking shape. Many were impressive, worth exhibiting. The intuitive and creative talents of our people never ceases to amaze me.

In the middle of the class I caught myself feeling normal until I thought about the lump in my stomach.

When I got home at 1:30, I called the clinic. The nurse informed me that Doctor Marioka was out ill but that Dr. LeBaron could see me at 2:30.

After having my vital signs taken and weighing in at 165 pounds, I was let into the examining room. A few minutes later, Doctor LeBaron cheerfully walked in. After the normal questions I mentioned losing ten pounds in the last six months but attributed it to all the work done while moving our home and the stress from leaving my job at Stanford University. He asked what I did—"Free-lance writer and artist." He stopped writing, turned to look at me and leaned back on his chair, "Burciaga! You were at Casa Zapata!"

"I'm familiar with your departure from Stanford. I've never heard of anything like that. I was dismayed by what happened to you and your wife, Cecilia."

After twenty years, Cecilia's position had been eliminated at Stanford University under the guise of budget cuts. The ensuing student protests and hunger strikes blamed politics under a new, conservative, German-born president, a Republican African-American woman provost and an African- American Dean. The multiculturalization of conservative politics was used to oust the high-ranking Mexican-American administrator at Stanford.

We talked briefly about Stanford and then Doctor LeBaron studied my lump, moved it and poked at it. "Hmm . . ." he said, and "very interesting." You can always tell how serious an illness is by the number of "hmms . . ." and "very interesting" comments.

"It's movable, so it can't be an organ . . . could be a cyst . . ." He called in another doctor, who also said, "Hmm . . . very interesting."

I was sent to the Stanford University Hospital Diagnostics Center for ultra-sound photo images. After parking and locking the car, I noticed an attractive blonde woman wearing a white smock who was walking ahead of me. She was gently carrying a beautiful bouquet of flowers and entered the same building I was headed to.

Inside, the receptionist directed me to the basement floor of the X-ray department, where the attractive blonde woman greeted me. The flowers had disappeared. She had me lie down on the examining table and then began to record the ultra-sound images of the lump and my abdomen.

She spent half an hour studying the lump on the monitor with a few "hmms" and a couple of "oopses" trying to get the machine to respond. Finally she called in another doctor who spent a few minutes studying the screen and massaging the paddle over my abdomen.

They wouldn't talk in front of me, but I caught the word "cyst" and they talked about the problem they were having getting an image of my pancreas. A cat scan was needed. Yes, there was a massive growth, but more they couldn't tell.

It was late Thursday, and no further openings were available in the schedule for cat scans. There was nothing else to be done but wait until Monday. I went home with two bottles of barium, one to drink Sunday night and the second for Monday morning, before the cat scan.

I called Margarita that night. We had been out of touch for a few days.

She wasn't feeling well. Her rheumatoid arthritis was torturing her, and at times she could barely move. She was worried and her voice was strained, as she said, "The arthritic pain in my shoulder is so severe it feels like a fracture. My pain medication isn't working anymore."

Despite her arthritis, Margarita had been going non-stop the whole year, teaching, starting a ballet folklórico group, helping launch a major "Viva El Paso" production and helping her son Aaron's soccer team. Margarita was an outstanding teacher of Spanish, Mexican history, culture and ethics. She was known for her kind but tough fairness, and did not tolerate chewing gum or misconduct in her classroom.

I felt helpless upon hearing her troubles. Though I was going to keep my condition quiet until I was certain what it was, I decided to tell her. Perhaps by sharing, she would not feel so alone. It helped some, but then again, I only added to her problems. I quickly swore her to secrecy until after the cat scans because I didn't want to alarm anyone needlessly.

Margarita became very concerned. We talked about how quickly we begin expecting the worst. As a single mother with a 14-year-old, Margarita dreaded anything happening to her.

At the end of the day when I discovered the tumor, I began to write a journal. I felt the urgent need to write down what was happening:

I don't know what I'm supposed to feel, but I have thought of it as a death sentence, as terminal . . . But I have never thought "Why me?" Hell no! I know why me.! Just because! Just because this is the way life is. You have to go sometime. But the first thing that enters your mind is leaving your family. I don't want to leave my family. I feel like a complete part of my family. As a father, I have that responsibility.

But I'm not too sure about what I have, or if it is terminal. I must not dwell on the negative. I have to fight back and continue living like I have. I don't want things to change just because I may be ill.

I see the challenge before me and I admire everyone who has died like this, knowing they are terminally ill . But maybe I'm not dying at all. Although I have believed that living is the process of dying. Even before this I have thought of death a great deal, written about it and some days I have said to myself, "Well, I am one day closer to death."

I haven't told Cecilia. But earlier in the day, before calling for an appointment, I did call to ask her if we still had the same medical insurance since moving from Stanford. We did. I told her about the lump. She said, "How strange," and then I blew it off by saying, "You know how I am, but I might as well get it checked out."

Tomorrow I will tell her. Tonight she is with Rebeca, and I will not hit them with a bombshell. It might be nothing, nothing, nothing. Why worry them needlessly?

I called Efrain, my brother in Long Beach but didn't mention anything.

It's 9:15. I just wanted to write this down today . . . for posterity? I have to look up that word. Words change meaning within the compression of time.

Friday
16 December

Toño woke up on his own, aware he can no longer depend on me to wake him up. I thought of saying something to him about my condition but I didn't want to blurt something out so early in the morning and maybe spoil his weekend.

During the night I awoke at 3:30 and kept waking up,

realizing I'm carrying something that has to be exorcised. My only fear at this point is telling Cecilia. During the day, I tried calling Cecilia twice but left no message.

When Cecilia came home Friday night, I didn't have the heart to tell her everything. I had cooked a green chile chicken *pozole.* Earlier in the day I had found a bottle of good champagne, put it in the fridge and pulled it out when Cecilia came home. This celebration drink would help break the bad news.

We caught up on the events of the week and in between I mentioned how Doctor LeBaron who had examined me, recognized our name and immediately knew our Stanford story, how dismayed he had been by it all and . . . "yes, they did find something inside of me, a little cyst or tumor." Cecilia's eyes lit up with concern. I felt I had to diminish it so I continued to play it down, "It's probably a little cyst or tumor. I have to go in Monday for a cat scan.

Cecilia's immediate response was, "cat scans are for the head." She had not forgotten two close Stanford colleagues she lost to brain tumors.

Having always been honest with Cecilia, I felt guilty playing down the seriousness of my situation, lying to her when the doctor had mentioned the "massive spread of cysts, a tumor or something . . ."

Friday night, I had a nightmare within a dream. In my dream I was having nightmares. The bathroom toilet flushed by itself but I was confused and thought it was the rustling of leaves by a strong wind though it was December, when the trees sound like a closet full of empty clothes hangers.

In my dream I moved closer to Cecilia in bed and wanted to nudge her awake but she was fast asleep. I didn't want to wake her up. Toño's voice came through the door. I went to him and saw an older Toño, not the eighteen-year-old. I remembered my plea to God, that He let Toño grow old. Maybe this was the trade-off. "Fair enough," I thought, "but please give me at least six more months to complete some work"

I awoke from one dream after another like petals falling from a flower, one after another, peelings after peelings, plunging me into a more surrealistic reality, or realistic surreality.

The next morning Rosa Apodaca called. She had run into Luz Herrera and they had exchanged concerns about my weight loss. I kept quiet about my condition.

Rosa was also concerned about the violence among Chicano youth in Santa Cruz. A young male student was approached about whether he was Norteño or Sureño. He blew it off and got in a fight with a couple of cholos. He was big, knew boxing and was able to defend himself. But a week later he was stabbed. The student survived, but barely.

"Well," I said to Rosa, "My daughter Rebeca and a group of friends drove to a 7-11 convenience store in a safe part of Santa Cruz. She was with four or five young Chicana women and one African-American guy.

"This cholo came up to the rider side of the car and asked the black guy if he was Norteño or Sureño."

Rosa interrupted, "Pendejo! Couldn't he tell the guy was a southerner?"

The black guy didn't answer so the cholo swung at him through the window. The car screeched out of the parking space as the cholo began to pull something out of his back pocket. Everyone expected a gun. But it was a long police flashlight. He threw it at the front windshield and it shattered. Fortunately, Rebeca was not driving her own car.

"We have to do something, the community has to get involved and know about this." Rosa said angrily.

A suspect was already in custody but the students were afraid to testify in an open court hearing. These cholos were gang members, with connections, vengeance squads and an "¿Y que?", "So what?" attitude.

Police warned Rebeca not to drive her car around the town. Fortunately, she had already planned to be with her Tía Margarita in El Paso for the next semester.

Saturday,
17 December

I have to tell Cecilia everything today. We are supposed to drive to her parents house in Southern California on the 22nd of December. At this point, I don't know what the doctors will decide. Start treatment right away, operate? Doctor LeBaron will be gone. Dr. Marioka will be back but they will probably turn me over to a surgeon.

By telling Cecilia, I hope to build some strength for Rebeca and Toño. I want things to continue normally. If we stop living normally, we will lose ground with reality and the purpose of life.

A week after my discovery, at the suggestion of Margarita, I lit a votive candle to Our Lady of Guadalupe and so did Cecilia in her Monterey home. We were separated and all four of us were driving back and forth. I had always wanted to light votive candles but ever since our kids were little I have always been afraid of lit candles in our house. I carefully set the votive candle in front of the fire place.

I wrote in my journal:

Today I thought, "¡Dios es grande!"—God is great!

I was born from my parents and I will be reborn to my parents in death.

I will return to God, I will return to eternity

I will embark on the greatest adventure, death itself.

Death is a miracle.

From something I will return to nothing.

But I will leave a place that occupies no space.

I look forward to death as I looked forward to birth.

But with faith, I am not afraid.

Imagination is so powerful I can think this is nothing but imagination. And so it is.

As I write, words bloom and blossom like flowers unfolding their petals into truth, shapes and meanings, definitions I took for granted. My soul now has 20-20 vision. Words were once metaphors and today they return to metaphorical beauty.

Xochipilli, príncipe de flores, Dios de la primavera, santo patrón de floricantos, poesía, música, danza y teatro!—Sochipili, prince of flowers, god of spring, patron saint of flower songs, poetry, music, dance and theater. The Náhuatl language is comprised of metaphors, not words.

For the Náhuas, flowers were a manifestation of life, being the birth of life, the first stage in the development of fruit, the sustenance of life. To the Náhuas, words were flowers, metaphors that gave birth to thoughts and actions. Poets affirmed the reality of beauty through flowers and song as the path to the knowledge of truth and a fountain of joy and friendship.

22 December

After five days, I write again. I have passed the stage from a journal keeper to a very mortal person, tempered by the knowledge that the diagnosis was serious enough to warrant an operation as soon as possible.

Five days ago I could have written about the details, who said what, where and how. Those details no longer seem important.

Doctor Harry Oberhelman, chief surgeon of the gastroenterology department and a renowned international specialist, took my case, perhaps due to the tumor's size and rarity. He exuded warmth and confidence as he illustrated and explained the numerous and overwhelming cat scan X-rays on the lit wall. The massive tumor was projected again and again in each image, pushing against the stomach, the pancreas, enveloping the spleen and pushing against the diaphragm. In the end I asked, "Is it cancer? Is it malignant?" He looked straight at me "Yes, we have to take it out soon."

I still had a cold so they couldn't operate. They prescribed an antibiotic and scheduled an operation for December 28. Doctor O. explained everything plainly and clearly, but his words refused to make contact with my reality. I wasn't denying it. It just wasn't registering. Another world embraced me after that. I did not feel the shock or fear of a death sentence. This new world was kind and accepting.

Down the corridor, into the elevator, through the lobby, I dreaded calling Cecilia. Better now than later, get it over with. Two public telephones waited in the lobby. I carefully picked one and dialed.

Cecilia was waiting for my call. Swelled with emotion I dialed and choked through my words to tell her the diagnosis. Cecilia was silently pained but strong, the conversation short. She immediately called Rosa, her sister.

At home I casually mentioned my upcoming operation to Rebeca and Toño. " . . . small operation to remove a small tumor." Their reaction was just what I needed. They must have been concerned but they didn't show it and instead asked which one would inherit the computer. To laugh at death brought back memories of my father, who would ask his children if we would die anytime we were ill. When he got sick we would ask him what color he preferred his casket. "Bright orange" he would answer.

Cecilia talked with Doctor Oberhelman, who said, "The

scan shows the tumor displacing organs and pushing on the stomach. It pushes against the diaphragm, pancreas, liver, colon. It is probably malignant. Portions of the liver, pancreas, colon and stomach may have to be removed but he has reserves and this should not cause organ problems."

At that point Doctor O. thought it was a sarcoma tumor, which vary in degree of malignancy. The more of these, the denser and more malignant it will be. There was also the possibility of it being lymphoma. A large and hard tumor with lesions of this nature usually turns out to be malignant.

They would remove the tumor and immediately do a biopsy. A radiologist would be present during the operation, ready to direct radiation into malignant areas before sewing me back up. I had agreed to a risky procedure that could cause another cancer.

During this time I awakened at every level of the day with insights about life and death that I never had before. I realized our only truthful connection in this world after severing the umbilical cord is God. I see no one else coming close at this stage but that higher level after life most of us believe in.

My parents' voices echo back to me in words I often heard them say: "Dios es grande." Words continue to open up like budding flowers as I open my soul and spirit wider than I thought possible.

Am I worried, Rebeca and Toño ask me? No. Scared? I don't think so. I feel more sorrow to leave the dearest people I have on earth.

I've had a good life. Fifty-four years is a good chunk. Cecilia, the kids and I have had a good family life. But I'm getting ahead of myself. I could pull through. My words are still guided by intuition. I must remember that faith is not faith without positive thinking.

I felt removed from the world, looking at it more critically. I thought of Joe Lopez, my sister Connie's late boyfriend, who said, "I don't need this shit in my life." Who does?

I called Margarita to tell her the diagnosis, tried to soften it, but she understood the severity.

Margarita's health had deteriorated and her voice was weak, teeming with pain. The doctor decided to hospitalize her. Margarita and I were more concerned with each other than ourselves. I hung up the telephone and wept on Cecilia's shoulder

Cecilia and I began asking friends for their prayers for Margarita and myself. There wasn't much time, but we called relatives and friends, especially those whom we saw as spiritual leaders in the community.

23 December

As we drove down to Southern California, I was emotionally inebriated, nursing a cold, a barium hangover and iodine injections in my veins.

Driving through the soft velvet hills of Northern California, Cecilia and I enjoyed each other's company and we made some decisions, including a no-mess, no-fuss cremation. Though it might not turn out to be necessary, we had to prepare for the worst while leading our lives as normally as possible. Toño and Rebeca drove down in a separate car because from their grandparents place they would go on to Texas, where Rebeca would visit and study for one semester at the University of Texas at El Paso.

Christmas 1994 was not normal. Nor is it ever any other year. Christmas is the most emotion-packed season despite the tinsel and glitter. Capitalism does a great job of obscuring the true spirit of Christmas.

On the 24th, I had one last Christmas gift to buy for *mi cuñada* Rosa, my sister-in-law. The moment I walked into the bookstore I was drawn to a shelf of best sellers, and my eyes focused in on a small thin paperback entitled, "Embraced by the Light," a real-life account of an after-death experience. The cover was too hokey, too religious. I was claiming to be more spiritual than religious. But I decided to at least pick it up and leaf through it. Almost embarrassed at buying it, I read the whole book that day and found it spiritually inspiring on the eve of my operation.

Christmas *con mis suegro's,* my in-laws, was too tense for me this time. I blew up at Rosa and went to bed ruining the day for everyone. The next morning, before returning home with Cecilia I apologized to her. She understood the pressure I was under. Toño and Rebeca drove on to El Paso.

The 26th of December I spent in my studio, clearing paperwork, correspondence and bills late into the night.

I entered the hospital on the 27th and almost burst my battered stomach, drinking a gallon of laxative in four hours. I continued calling a few more friends asking for their prayers, not only for me but for Margarita also: Father Eugene Boyle, a veteran United Farm Workers activist;

Tenaxtli, an indigenous Aztec dance and prayer group from San Juan Bautista; Cid Flores, a Chicano-Chumash Indian attorney from San José, married to Anecita, a Navaho woman and her mother, Pima; Andrés Segura, an old friend and an elder Aztec healer from Mexico City; Stanford Law Professor Miguel Mendez; Dan Ramirez, a Pentecostal "Alleluya" as he likes to call himself, also offered his prayers, as did nuns in El Paso, former Stanford students, some of their parents, and Jewish friends. My sister Lupe, who was traveling through Italy, prayed at the tomb of Saint Anthony of Padua. The list seemed endless.

On the morning of the 28th, I was awake when the nurses and anesthesiologist came to my room at seven in the morning. The chief anesthesiologist was Doctor Rick Ronquillo, who nine years earlier had lived with us in Casa Zapata as a Stanford undergraduate. Later, as a medical student he had served as an undergraduate advisor. Rick had requested this case because he knew my family and wanted to help.

The operation lasted four hours. A ten-pound tumor, the size and color of a beige desk telephone was extracted. Doctor O. had found it necessary to take part of my stomach, part of my pancreas, all of my spleen and cut into my diaphragm. He gave Ronquillo the assignment of informing Cecilia of the operation's success.

In the split second instant, just before opening my eyes in the intensive care unit after the operation I felt a flash of light. It was stronger than the fluorescent lights, more than a visual light. And at that very moment I had a mysterious but absolute knowledge that I was alright. Nothing more was wrong with me. My spirit was talking for me, to me, with me and through me.

Besides the 12-inch stapled incision, I had three tubes in my nose (two for oxygen and one to drain my stomach), two tubes drained my abdominal area, another from the side of my lung, one IV needle went into my arm, another for I don't remember what. An epidural needle was in my spine for anesthesia, and a catheter went up to my bladder.

People began to prepare me for an even rougher road ahead, chemotherapy and radiation. Journalist friends, Bob Beyers and Mary Madison, took a personal interest from their own experiences and provided me with information about my condition. This fortified me.

José Cuellar, alias Dr. Loco, the musician, socio-anthropologist and head of Chicano Studies at San Francisco State along with his wife, Stacy, were my first visitors. José presented me with a bouquet of brightly colored paper flowers his mother had made. For the ancient Mexicanos, paper flowers were the insignia of the gods or the sacrificed.

After two days in intensive care, I was put in a regular hospital room filled with bouquets of flowers, pots of flowers and plants.

I called Margarita. Her voice was no better than mine, weak, soft, pained. We were barely able to talk to each other.

I received many visitors, and at night doctors, nurses or technicians stopped by every two hours. Despite the tiring 24-hour attention from friends and nurses, I couldn't complain. Each individual visit represented a prayer, a good thought, positive energy.

"I need some pajamas from home," I told Cecilia. But she insisted on buying a new pair from an after-Christmas sale. She returned to the hospital with a new pair of light yellow pajamas with prints of cowboy boots. I couldn't afford to laugh, it was the one thing I dreaded . . . but I couldn't help it and I began to laugh. They were hilarious and it hurt.

That night was the most restless and painful. My temperature shot up, I hallucinated, and was given two units of blood.

Cecilia had already notified my brothers and sisters. Meanwhile, Margarita was getting worse. X-rays had discovered cancer in her lungs. How much or how little it was hard to tell, they didn't know or they weren't telling Cecilia and me.

By the fifth day in the hospital no one had washed me and I was helpless. My hair was matted down, my bed sheets were stained and not been changed in three days. With a nurse or technician coming by every two hours, I began asking but their answers became all too familiar, "I'm sorry sir, but my job is . . ."

I finally decided not to co-operate with the next person, who happened to be an African-American woman who looked like a loving mother. "I'm sorry sir, but I'm just here to take your vital signs." I began to argue but realized her strength and determination. I let her take my temperature and blood pressure in defeated silence.

After finishing, she said, "I'll be right back to help you."

Expecting an assistant, if anybody, she returned in 15 minutes and helped me sit in a chair. After changing my bed sheets, the woman filled a plastic container and bathed me with a wash cloth. I appreciated feeling clean again. Those smug daily showers of warm water that once woke my body seemed so long ago.

Finally, she filled a small plastic tub with warm water and placed my feet inside as she knelt down and began to clean them. It was more than I had expected. My misery had put me at the kind mercy of her charity. Feeling my pain and disabled condition I choked up in an attempt to thank her. Jesus Christ had done this to his apostles. Mary Magdalene had cleaned Christ's feet with her tears and long hair.

"Now, don't you go crying on me!" The woman admonished. She dried my feet and helped me back to bed.

The next day, Doctor O. stopped by my bed with the prognosis, " . . .after consulting with a "tumor board" of oncologists and other specialists, we have decided that we got everything out and you don't need chemotherapy or radiation. The possibility of recurrence is almost non-existent."

This confirmed what I had first known upon waking up from the operation. That had been the miracle, but I hadn't recognized it for certain. For the past four days I had put it in the back of my mind, telling no one, not wanting to be overly optimistic.

Margarita's condition worsened, improved and then worsened again. She was sent home for a few days, felt better and then began to deteriorate and returned to the hospital. Details on her condition were sketchy. I understood why we weren't getting the full story on her condition.

I continued to have fascinating dreams: "I'm facing what looks like the Great Canyon. On the other side of one canyon, young *Mexicanos* approach the edge intent on crossing the big divide. They carefully slide, leap and jump down from one rock precipice to another, but eventually there are no more levels and I witness many bodies plunging down, helplessly falling, their arms and legs flailing, plummeting down beyond to where I cannot see—death."

My friend Irma Meza urged me to think about those dreams as messages.

Oscar, Margarita's 18-year-old-son had a dream one night in Mexico City before going home to see his mother. Oscar dreamed of a big fiesta but the only people he recognized were his grandparents and his mother. The others were older people he had known as a child. That same day, Margarita woke up in the hospital complaining about the number of visitors she had the night before. "Everybody was here," said Margie, "my parents and tías!"

I returned home from the hospital. Positive energy flowed our way through visitors, prayers, good wishes, thoughts, cards and flowers. This created a house of flowers, a house of springtime, of life. Bernice Zamora brought me a poem, known in ancient Mexico as a *sartal de flores,* a string of flowers.

Irma reminded me to pray in the way of our indigenous ancestors, to the four directions. I remembered how our grandmother prayed to the four directions. Every day from Juarez, Chihuahua, she would face Los Angeles, and then Chicago, where her children lived, and pray for them.

"Pray not only to your parents" Cid Flores suggested, "but to your grandparents and great-great-grandparents, all the way back to the beginning of time; Stand on Mother Earth, give her the weakness and pain in your knees and receive her energy." We burned sage, prayed to the four directions and felt the softness of Mother Earth under our feet."

Very slowly, day by day, I got stronger while Margie got weaker. Rebeca was by Margie's side, along with Aaron, her cousins, Patricia and Cathy, and my sisters, Lupe and Connie. Norman Luján, Margie's former husband, a nurse at that hospital and former Vietnam veteran was by her side day and night. I called and talked to Aaron, who cried as I tried to contain myself and comfort him.

I also wanted to talk to Margie. We were so very close, and now I couldn't even talk to her. Her eyes were closed, but she could hear so Rebeca placed the telephone to her ear and, trying to control my emotions, I yelled, "Margarita! This is Tony! I love you! I want you to know that I'm going to dedicate my next book to you!"

"You should come down," Rebeca told me, "She's close to the end."

But I didn't know if I could travel. I was still too weak and I tired easily.

In the hospital, Margie's condition got worse. One day she lunged up in bed, her eyes jutting out in desperation.

She couldn't breathe. She was given additional morphine. Her lungs were perforated and filling up with liquid. Desperately she hung on to life, trying at least to wait for the arrival of Oscar, but it was too painful and difficult.

Rebeca finally asked Aaron, "Tell your mother to rest now. It's okay!"

Aaron went to his mother's side, "Mom, It's okay! You can rest now!"

Moments later Margarita rested peacefully. Margarita, with the name of a beautiful flower had died.

We flew down for the rosary, the mass and the burial. I dreaded the grieving and facing Oscar and Aaron. I was certain I would break down in tears, but the moment I saw Aaron's smiling strength I was inspired to laugh with joy.

It was the same with Oscar, who had arrived two hours after her passing. My brothers came, Raul from Albuquerque, Efrain and his dear friend Jeannie from Long Beach. Connie from Mazatlán had been at Margarita's side the whole month.

Marty, Raul's wife, was a funeral director and took care of all the burial arrangements. I had always thought it a strange and morbid profession until I saw and heard of the great help Marty provided to grieving Mexican immigrants and their families in Albuquerque. Today she was helping us, immigrants on this earth.

The grieving funerals I had known as a child disappeared. This was a celebration of life, a resurrection to eternal life. A teacher for twenty years, many of Margarita's teaching colleagues and students were present.

Mount Carmel Cemetery, close to the Río Grande, is in the middle of a bare but populated desert. All the tombs, without exception, had beautifully colored paper and plastic flowers, insignias of the ancient Aztec gods and the sacrificed. Hundreds of flowers, as far and wide as the cemetery decorated the dry yellow grass.

"How come?" I asked.

"Real flowers don't last long in the desert," Cecilia reminded me. Like flowers, we also don't last long in this desert called life.

Mariachis played for Margarita. They played tunes she danced as a young woman. I asked them to play "Margarita" and they ended with "Las Golondrinas," the traditional farewell song.

As I write this, the last days of February 1995 are passing. After a cold, wet and gray January, the weather is glorious this week, the sun-filled blue skies are serenaded by swarms of birds returning and the trees blossom in soft colors. The beige hills of December are now lush green. White and yellow Margaritas bloom everywhere.

The white and pink tree blossoms dream of the fruit they will bear in the spring. In the earth, seeds are sowed for future dreams and flowers, our sustenance.

Margarita's life was like a flower, ephemeral but beautiful, here for an instant and gone too soon. But she left the fragrance of her memory as she continues to live through Oscar, Aaron, her brothers, sisters, the people she loved and knew, the students she taught, the things she touched . . .